# THE *Spirituality*
# OF PETS

*Dogs are our link to paradise.*
*They don't know evil or*
*jealousy or discontent.*
*To sit with a dog on a hillside*
*on a glorious afternoon is*
*to be back in Eden,*
*where doing nothing was not boring*
*— it was peace.*

– Milan Kundera, czech novelist

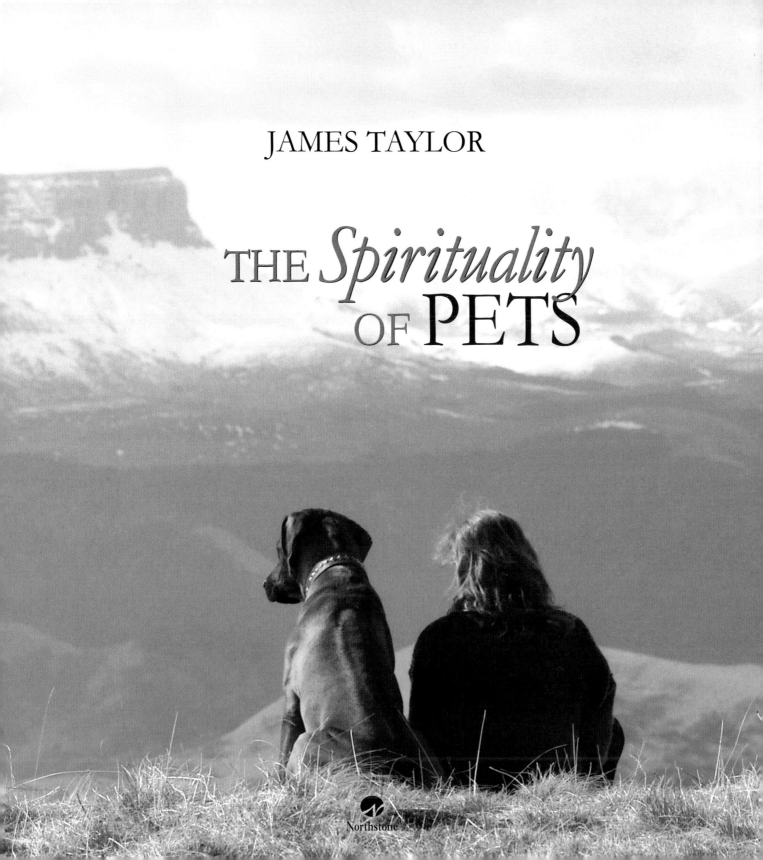

JAMES TAYLOR

THE *Spirituality* OF PETS

Northstone

Concept: Northstone Team
Editor: Tim Faller
Industry Consultant: Darcy Bomford from Darford Industries:
    Pet Food/Treat Manufacturer
Cover: Margaret Kyle
Interior design: Margaret Kyle and Verena Velten
Proofreading: Dianne Greenslade
Photo credits: see page 160

**Northstone** is an imprint of **Wood Lake Publishing, Inc.** Wood Lake Publishing acknowledges the financial support of the Government of Canada, through the Book Publishing Industry Development Program (BPIDP) for its publishing activities.

At Wood Lake Publishing, we practice what we publish, being guided by a concern for fairness, justice, and equal opportunity in all of our relationships with employees and customers. Wood Lake Publishing is an employee-owned company, committed to caring for the environment and all creation. Wood Lake Books recycles, reuses, and encourages readers to do the same. Resources are printed on 100% post-consumer recycled paper and more environmentally friendly groundwood papers (newsprint), whenever possible. A percentage of all profit is donated to charitable organizations.

**Library and Archives Canada Cataloguing in Publication**
Taylor, James, 1936-
The spirituality of pets / James Taylor.
Includes bibliographical references.
ISBN 1-896836-81-X
1. Pets. 2. Spirituality. I. Title.
BT746.T39 2006          636.088'7          C2006-902428-6

Published by Northstone
9590 Jim Bailey Road, Kelowna, BC V4V 1R2 Canada
www.northstone.com
250.766.2778


Printing 10 9 8 7 6 5 4 3 2 1
Printed in China

*One must ask children and birds how cherries and strawberries taste.*

– Johann Wolfgang von Goethe

# Contents

# 1
# Setting the Stage

INTRODUCTION TO THE CONCEPTS AND CHARACTERS OF THIS BOOK

When I started writing this book about the spirituality of pets, my hardest task was to excavate down through the layers of presumptions that I made about pets. I had lots of stories about pets, and about animals in general. Everyone does. I took for granted that they had something they could teach me – about nature, about God, about myself. Not until I started gathering those stories together and organizing them did I become aware of the questions they raised, as well as the questions they answered.

*Dogs are not our whole life, but they make our lives whole.*

– ROGER CARAS, BROADCASTER, AUTHOR, ANIMAL-RIGHTS ACTIVIST

For example, do pets know God?

I mean, if pets are simply a flesh-and-bone package for DNA trying to prolong its own survival – a sort of biological robot that has found in our homes a life support system that gives them an advantage over non-pets – they're not likely to have much to teach us about a universal divinity that loves unconditionally.

So I have to go back, to ask myself: What are pets?

Why do we have them?

And then, further: What's their relationship with God? And what's God's relationship with them?

Only then can I ask: How can they affect my relationship with God, with others, and with myself? And how can they teach us, if they don't speak our language?

## CAST OF CHARACTERS

Although I don't limit this book to my own pets, they are the dominant characters in it, so you might as well meet them. Over the years, my wife, Joan, and I have shared our homes and lives with five cats and three dogs.

Our first cat was Tuppence, a tortoiseshell tabby. She was just a few weeks old when we picked her out of a litter at a farm. We had asked for an orange-and-white cat, but when Tuppence came out from under the barn, with her multi-coloured coat, we fell in love with her.

The farm family had named her Jane. My mother thought "Plain Jane" didn't suit, and casually muttered a phrase recalled from childhood: "Penny plain and tuppence coloured." From that moment on, her name was Tuppence.

Tuppence had a litter of six kittens. We kept one, a black-and-white cat who looked almost exactly like the cartoon cat Sylvester. Sylvester died of liver cancer before he was five.

When Tuppence died, at 19½, our daughter, Sharon, decided that we needed a replacement. Or two. Through a friend, she found us two sisters, also tortoiseshell tabbies. We called one of them Spice because

*I love cats because I enjoy my home; and little by little, they become its visible soul.*

– JEAN COCTEAU, FRENCH POET

she was all the colours of spices – cinnamon, pepper, traces of Dijon mustard, coriander, sage, thyme… We thought we would name her sister Sugar, so that we would have Sugar and Spice. But Sharon's friend had already named her Mush, because when she got any cuddling from humans, she turned as limp as mush.

Spice lived to be 15. As I write this book, Mush is still going at 18.

## The Lucky Ones

Our current youngest cat is Lucky. We didn't really want another cat, but I felt some responsibility for this one. Because I ran over her with the car.

I was driving past an orchard when a little grey cat dashed out from the trees, racing across the road in front of me with that peculiar grace of a feline in full flight.

I slammed on the brakes. I swerved. The front wheels missed her. I was just beginning to breathe a prayer of relief when something went thump under the car's rear end.

I looked back. A small blob of fur was struggling to raise herself off the asphalt. She blew bright red bubbles of blood out of her nose.

Taking her gently in my arms, I tried to find her home. "Not mine," said the first man brusquely, and closed the door.

She didn't belong to the folks on the other side of the road either, where the cat had come from, but they wiped the blood off her face and

called the vet's office, on the chance he might be working late. He was.

"Bring her in," Dr. Eliot Kaplan told me.

I phoned the next morning. "She's still alive," said Tracy at the clinic. "But we think her head injuries have left her blind."

Over the next two weeks, the clinic advertised for the little cat's owner. I visited every house along that stretch of road. When both searches proved fruitless, I felt so guilty that I took the unfortunate creature myself.

"She's lucky to have you," said Tracy.

So that became her name – Lucky.

Lucky still can't see much; she cannot constrict the pupils in her eyes. But she has learned to get around our house without bumping into things or falling down the stairs. She trots happily along beside my large shoes. She climbs into our laps and purrs. She even chases birds occasionally.

If she's lucky, so are we.

*The cat has too much spirit to have no heart.*

– Ernest Menaul

*I've always thought*
*a hotel ought to offer*
*optional small animals.*
*I mean a cat to sleep*
*on your bed at night,*
*or a dog of some kind to act*
*pleased when you come in.*
*You ever notice how*
*a hotel room feels so lifeless?*

– ANNE TYLER, PULITZER PRIZE-WINNING NOVELIST

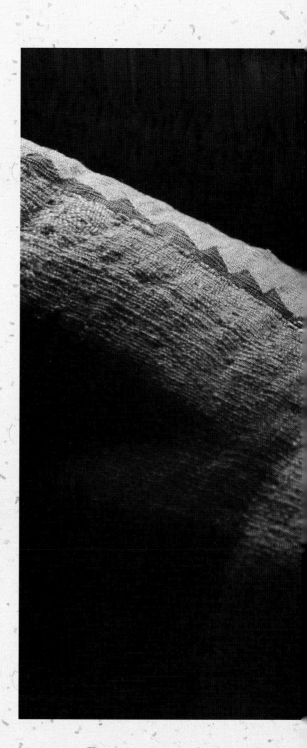

Joan and I had been married less than a year when I stopped by the Vancouver dog pound on my way home one night, and fell for a bright-eyed flop-eared fox terrier named Mickey. He was about a year and a half old at the time, and the happiest dog I have ever known.

Tragically, we had to have him put down when he was about five, because my job moved us to a new city, into an apartment that did not permit pets. I still regret that decision, over 40 years later.

We didn't feel it was fair to have a dog while we lived in urban Toronto for 25 years. Not until we moved back to a rural area in B.C. in 1993 did we feel free to have a dog again. Joan was looking in the local newspaper one Sunday morning when she came across a picture of the SPCA's "Pet of the Week."

"Here's an Irish setter," said Joan. "They're not very big, are they?"

I've always had a soft spot for the breed. They look so gorgeous. So I picked up the phone and called the SPCA. "Is that Irish setter still available?"

We came home with a purebred Irish setter, Irishfleet's Brickendorn – Brick for short. That first night, Brick didn't want to let us out of his sight. I succeeded in convincing him not to climb onto the bed with us, but during the night he managed to knock over the lamp, my glasses, my alarm clock, and Joan's picture.

When I woke, he had one hind leg sticking up through a lampshade.

Brick, as you'll read later, taught me an enormous amount about

*No matter how little money and how few possessions you own, having a dog makes you rich.*

– LOIUS SABIN, AUTHOR

myself, and about my ability to love – to love him, to love anyone. He died at the age of ten of multiple complications – a lifetime of epileptic seizures, hip dysplasia, a damaged back…

## HEALING PRESENCE

We grieved for Brick for almost a year. We considered getting another dog, but couldn't face doing it. Then, one afternoon, a friend called. "Do you know anyone who might like to adopt an Irish setter?"

Three hours later, we were headed home with Phoebe in the back seat of our car. Instantly, our home felt whole again. She wasn't the same big red furball, but she *was* a big red furball.

In spite of love at first sight, we had some qualms about taking Phoebe. She was already ten. That meant she probably didn't have too long to live. Then we thought, if we could have had Brick for another year or two, would we have hesitated? Emphatically not! So we adopted Phoebe.

She has been an absolute joy. She's gentle, trusting, quiet, patient, placid, and loyal. And she's beautiful. The way she dances down the road for her morning walk would make Ginger Rogers look awkward.

Phoebe is almost 13 now, a remarkable age for an Irish setter. She too has taught me a great deal.

An elderly friend, Honor Halliday, once told me that she takes Phoebe as her role model. "She never complains," explained Honor.

"She's always cheerful. At her age, her joints must hurt sometimes, like mine, but she doesn't let that stop her from enjoying her walks. She loves everyone, and she's confident that everyone loves her. What more could anyone ask?"

## Supporting Actors

Other animals will show up in these pages too, of course, for pets come in all varieties, and animals surround us no matter where we live. We have deer wandering through our yard here in B.C. In Toronto, it was raccoons. And we have always had squirrels and birds around.

But you will not find in these pages many references to books or to academic research. I've read those books, over the years. But my focus here is on how pets have affected my spirituality – and how I hope they can affect your spirituality – not on what you and I might learn from other authors. Much of their wisdom has sunk so deeply into my consciousness that I can no longer identify where it came from, anyway. So I have concentrated on the experiences, the stories, not on the research.

I hope that when you have finished reading this book, you will discover in your pets – and your other animal encounters – as rich a resource for your own spiritual development as I have.

## Role Plays

But if animals can't utter words, how can they teach anything? We humans have an obsession with words. We find it hard to imagine learning that doesn't take place in something like a classroom setting, with a professor lecturing from dry and dusty notes. Even in the family context, we think we have to impart wisdom to our children by explaining things in words.

We forget that children's most profound learning experiences take place before they have words to work with. The discovery of their own identity, of their parents, of their surroundings, of their toys, of their ability to roll over and crawl and perhaps stand up or even walk, typically precedes any verbal awareness.

As adults, we continue to be moved by music, by art, by a hug, or by a touch on the arm – and all of these can be utterly wordless.

I believe, therefore, God doesn't need to use words to give messages to us. Rather, God speaks to us in our experiences. The words come later, when we try to describe our experiences.

This notion actually came from our cat Mush.

*An animal's eyes have the power to speak a great language.*

– Martin Buber, philosopher

For 15 years, Joan had a job that required her to get out of bed by 6 a.m., Monday to Friday. The first thing she did was feed the cats, mostly to get them out from under her feet.

Mush knew, within a couple of minutes, when six o'clock came. She leaped onto our bed and climbed to the highest point of the covers – usually a hip – and there practiced the feline equivalent of yodelling.

If either of us happened to be lying on our back, she climbed aboard at about the ankles, and walked up the full length of our body. At mid-chest, she would stop, lean forward until her mouth was about an inch from our nose, and squawk: "Nyaouwwww!"

Have you ever smelled cat breath at 6 a.m.?

Mush didn't use words to communicate her message.

*If animals could speak,
the dog would be
a blundering
outspoken fellow;
but the cat would have
the rare grace
of never saying a word
too much.*

– MARK TWAIN

Humans have many languages. But the only thing all humans have in common is the experience of living.

We are born. We cry. We learn first to suckle, then to eat. We learn to crawl and to walk. We fall. We hurt ourselves. We are comforted. We are loved. We learn to love others. We grow up. We play. We work. (If we're lucky, we manage to do both at the same time.) We learn. Sometimes we grow wise. We certainly grow older. We lose our parents. We lose our teeth, our hearing, our memory. We lose our energy. We all lose some of our friends. We eventually lose our lives.

That's the universal story. And none of it requires words.

Some of the most poignant moments are, literally, wordless. Words would get in the way. One of our friends told us about holding her husband in her arms as he took his last breath. "He just got too tired to take another breath," she said. That's one such experience.

Do you remember falling hopelessly in love? Or feeling a newborn baby's hand close around your finger? Or watching your son or daughter come down the aisle for a wedding or a graduation? There is simply no room for words in the emotions of that moment.

At such times, it's the experience that matters, not the words. The words, if there are words at all, come later.

That's how I believe God speaks to us. And it is how God speaks to us through our pets.

## Are Animals Spiritual?

You may wonder: Can animals teach us about spirituality if they don't have spirituality themselves? I think that's a misleading question. It focuses on *their* experience, not ours. In truth, spirituality is never about someone else. It is always personal.

This is the fifth in a series of Northstone books on spirituality. Previous books have focused on the spirituality of wine, of mazes and labyrinths, of gardens, and of art. These things are all inanimate. But they influence, in one way or another, the spirituality of human beings. The same holds true for pets and other creatures. They may or may not have spirituality themselves – and by the way, I do think that many animals experience elements of awe and wonder, just as we do – but certainly their association with us affects *our* spirituality.

*People always joke that "dog" spells "god" backwards. They should consider that it might be the higher power coming down to see just how well they do, what kind of people they are.*
*The animals are right here, right in front of us. And how we treat these companions is a test.*

– LINDA BLAIR,
ACTRESS, ANIMAL ACTIVIST

# 2
# A Holy Imperative

RELATIONSHIPS WITH PETS REFLECT RELATIONSHIPS WITH THE DIVINE

Why do we have pets? The question occurred to me while watching a video clip on B.C.'s Knowledge Network, of some marine biologists with a seal who was doing some underwater research for them.

Seals are not natural friends of humans. Wild seals are – with good reason – suspicious of human intentions. Yet in this case, both the seal and the scientists were clearly enjoying their mutual relationship.

Personally, I can't pass a dog on the street without attempting to make friends with it. I have to restrain myself from taking home stray cats. For a while, I took snacks for a Muscovy duck living on the lake front – a domesticated bird that apparently preferred freedom to regular meals. At first, it flew away whenever I approached; before long, it waddled towards me on its big flat feet.

One of the greatest thrills of my life came on a trip to the Galapagos Islands, when our group was allowed to frolic in the ocean with wild sea lions. Their swimming skills simultaneously enchanted and humiliated us. When we left, a row of sleek heads stuck out of the water, as if saying, "Aw, do you have to go so soon?"

*A dog is the only thing on earth that loves you more than he loves himself.*

– JOSH BILLINGS, AMERICAN HUMOURIST

23

*Generally, or at least very often, people with a deep interest in animals are the best people around.*

– Roger Caras

Most of us, I suspect, have a deep desire to break down the barriers that divide us from the natural world. It's why debilitated seniors in care facilities will respond to a visiting pet. It's why dairy farmers get attached to their herds. It's why I catch my breath when a family of deer prance across my lawn, or a coyote saunters down the lane. For a short while, the barriers of suspicion and distrust that divide us come down.

Indeed, I have trouble relating to people who don't feel a sense of identification with animals. Driving home from church one Sunday morning, we encountered a pair of killdeer trying to chivvy their two little offspring off the road and into the safety of the ditch and the fields. The babies, tottering around on spindly little legs, showed no inclination to obey their parents.

The adults tried to call their babies to their side. It didn't work. They tried to shoo their babies to the other side. That didn't work either.

I felt a wave of sympathy for those killdeer parents, thinking how much killdeer families were like human families, when I realized that other cars on that country road were stacking up behind us. So I edged ahead, very slowly, hoping the looming presence of my car – which must seem like a behemoth to anything as tiny as a killdeer chick – would encourage the little ones to move to the side of the road.

Several cars going the other direction had also stopped to watch the minuscule domestic drama unfolding. At that moment, a car farther back in the line – a faded, rusted, red Ford Tempo – lost patience. Engine roaring in protest, the driver pulled out. He barely slowed down as he slalomed between the other vehicles on the road.

The killdeer family scattered in panic. I have no idea whether they ever reunited.

*It's difficult to understand why people don't realize that pets are gifts to mankind.*

– LINDA BLAIR, ACTRESS, INVOLVED IN
CHARITIES PREVENTING CRUELTY TO ANIMALS

*If I keep a green bough in my heart, the singing bird will come.*

– CHINESE PROVERB

Incidents like that fill me with a mix of hope and despair.

Hope – because there are still people who can take time out to experience the wonder of creation. In any contest between a killdeer and a car, the car will certainly win. But some of those drivers set themselves for a moment or two on the same level as a killdeer chick. They recognized that the chick has rights, too. It may well become a victim of a crow or a cat, but it doesn't have to be a victim of a Bridgestone tire.

And despair – because there are also people for whom such things don't matter at all. All that matters is their own immediate need. They have deliveries to make, appointments to keep, errands to complete. Anything that slows them down, that impedes their progress, is just an obstacle to be overcome.

If we humans have lost our sense of wonder when we deal with animals, are we likely to retain it when dealing with other humans?

Every religion has a teaching similar to the one our civilization calls the Golden Rule. Most English-speaking peoples know it best in the phrasing of the King James Version of the Bible: "Do unto others as you would have them do unto you" (Matthew 7:12). Although the words are attributed to Jesus, they were hardly new. A century before him, Judaism's Rabbi Hillel had stated it as, "What is hateful to you, do not do to your neighbour: that is the whole Torah; all the rest of it is commentary" (Talmud, Shabbat 31a).

Other formulations are similar. The Hindu Mahabharata puts it:

"One should not behave towards others in a way which is disagreeable to oneself." Confucius said, "Do not do unto others what you would not have them do unto you."

## A Broader Application

Western cultures tend to apply those instructions primarily to humans. Eastern religions, especially those that grew out of India, extend the concept to other creatures. If I dare interpret a faith that is not my own, by way of example, Hinduism believes in universal reincarnation. That is, after you die, you return to earth in some other form. Perhaps you move up the chain of evolutionary perfection, and become a priest or a cow. But if you have not lived an exemplary life, you might move down, perhaps returning as a monkey or a mongoose. So Hinduism offers a religious reason for treating non-human creatures with compassion. Because that sparrow might be your still-unborn great-grandson.

We in the secularized Western world don't have that motivation. Yet many of us still have an instinctive compulsion to be kind to animals.

When I went out to pick up our newspaper one morning, a shadow suddenly lurched to its feet. It was a dog I had never seen before, a rather mangy, moulting, black Labrador cross. I guess she had spent the night there, huddled on our driveway, in the dubious shelter of our boat.

Her tail was tucked so far between her legs that it looked glued to her belly. I could see a collar around her neck, and a dog tag hanging

*Ask of the beasts and they will teach you the beauty of this earth.*

– St. Francis of Assisi

28

from it, but she wouldn't let me come near enough to read the number so that I could trace her owner.

She was still there a couple of hours later. I assumed she had not had anything to drink for a while, so I took out a bucket of water. She backed away from me, baring her teeth. She knew what the bucket held. Even so, she wouldn't take a drink until I moved back. Then, her belly almost on the ground, she crept forward and started slurping.

As I watched her, a phrase about "a cup of cold water" came to mind. It comes from the gospel attributed to Matthew: "Whoever gives even a cup of cold water to one of these little ones…I tell you, none of these will lose their reward."

Jesus' parable of the sheep and the goats includes the instruction, "As you did it to one of the least of these…you did it to me." Does "the least of these" include stray dogs?

She disappeared during the afternoon. I thought she might merely have found some secluded spot, some shady hideaway from the heat of the day, so I put out some food for her that evening, in case she came back. But she never did.

Wherever she went, I hope she encountered kindness.

*Dogs are wise. They crawl away into a quiet corner and lick their wounds and do not rejoin the world until they are whole once more.*

– AGATHA CHRISTIE

*I think dogs
are the most
amazing creatures.
They give
unconditional love.
For me they are
the role model
for being alive.*

– GILDA RADNER, ACTRESS

I think that this desire to extend compassion to animals reflects our relationship with the divine. My tradition refers to the divine that lives in and among us as God; other traditions use other names. One of the primary teachings of my religious culture is that God offers unconditional love. Pets probably come as close to giving and receiving unconditional love as we can come in this flawed world.

Do you remember the schoolyard game of Tit for Tat? Usually, it meant retaliation: you punch me, and I'll punch you back. Nature, according to British biologist Lyall Watson, plays the game more altruistically. Somewhere in the genetic code of every creature is a predisposition to treat others as they have been treated so far. It's nature's form of the Golden Rule.

So until the other creature shows that it intends to harm you, you trust it. That's why human photographers can get so close to the rare white Kermode bears on B.C.'s most isolated coastal islands: the bears have not yet learned to be afraid of humans.

When strange dogs meet, before they decide on fight, flight, or friendship, they first sniff each other. Temple Grandin, in her book *Animals in Translation*, describes rats, Holstein cows, and wolves as super-curious creatures. "If I lie down in the middle of a pasture filled with Holsteins," she writes, "they'll come up and start licking my boots. They'll go up to a horse too, and start licking him on his backside."

One spring, our dog Brick and a duck demonstrated this tit for tat principle.

At first, Brick started off chasing the duck. She paddled away in panic. But gradually, she realized he was no threat; she could swim faster than he could. So they learned to swim along together. He waded

out and started swimming; she took up a position about an arm's length ahead of him.

Being an Irish setter, Brick had very little common sense. (One dog trainer described Irish setters as "so dumb they could get lost on the end of their own leash!") When he reached the end of his rope, he yelped loudly and beat the water into a froth with his front paws. Then he turned back to shore. The duck, instead of paddling away, turned around and accompanied him, swimming along just behind him.

Rudyard Kipling coined the phrase: "Nature red in tooth and claw..." But, in fact, it isn't. Nature has evolved an astonishingly sophisticated system of cooperation and, yes, even of trust. On a safari to Africa, I was amazed to see cheetahs and gazelles drinking from the same water hole. Or lions sunning themselves on a rocky outcrop while wildebeest grazed nearby. The prey animals are wary, but they co-exist with their predators. With rare exceptions, wild predators do not kill for the sake of killing. As long as there's an abundance of food available, they're prepared to live and let live.

It makes me wonder, sometimes, if the Hebrew prophet Isaiah had seen something similar, when he wrote about lions and lambs feeding together without fear.

Once, when Joan and I were snorkelling in the Galapagos Islands, we saw a shark swimming along the ocean floor, about 20 feet below us. Our first instinct was panic. Then we saw that other fish were not fleeing; the shark undulated peacefully among the brightly coloured reef fish. The shark was no threat to them – and therefore no threat to us.

Our own bodies are examples of this kind of coexistence. We live in a symbiotic relationship with the bacteria in our gut and on our skin. One biologist commented that if every cell that contained human DNA were somehow rendered invisible, a recognizably human shape would remain – composed entirely of bacteria! Far from being competitors, humans and "friendly bacteria" make each other's survival possible.

When we make friends with our pets, we fulfil a basic law of nature.

*Folks will know how large your soul is, by the way you treat a dog!*

– Charles F. Doran

All pet owners know that we have a special relationship with our pets. Few of these relationships last as long or travel as far as one I heard of – a woman who adopted a small land tortoise when she was a child in India, and still had it roaming her yard in Canada 60 years later! But the emotions don't depend on longevity.

We had had our little cat Lucky less than a year when she wandered off during the coldest snap of the winter. She went out one morning, and didn't come back.

For two days, we searched the district. We contacted neighbours. We posted notices. I covered our half-acre of garden on my hands and knees in the snow, peering into and under every bush and shrub where she might have taken refuge. When Joan finally found her and brought her home cuddled inside her parka, we rejoiced far more than eight pounds of fluff with a brain the size of my thumb would otherwise warrant.

More and more, as I grow older (and hopefully, wiser), I think that we humans are not individuals as much as we are relationships. It's not our height, or weight, or wealth that defines us as human beings. It's the range and depth of our relationships.

Old age is painful not just because of increasing disability, but because both the number and the quality of relationships necessarily declines. There can be few things lonelier than a 100-year-old man or woman who has outlived friends, siblings, colleagues, students, even children.

So I am more than a collection of limbs and organs. I am my relationships. In general, I feel extraordinarily gifted by those relationships, old and new. But I also feel poorer whenever one of those relationships comes to an end. That includes relationships with my pets.

I don't know when I have felt that loss more acutely than when our dog Brick died. His final days filled me with awe.

Brick was an Irish setter – a breed known for being scatterbrained, happy-go-lucky, and plagued by health problems. We don't know anything about his first year and a half, but from the time we got him, he had grand mal epileptic seizures every two months or so. He had a slipped disc in his spine. Like most large dogs, he suffered from hip dysplasia. In a previous bout with death, he had surgery for peritonitis from a ruptured duodenal ulcer; his belly was stitched from his groin to his breastbone.

*There is something about the presence of a cat... that seems to take the bite out of being alone.*

– LOUIS CAMUTI, VETERINARIAN, AUTHOR

35

Then a small tumour on his lip started bleeding all over our floors and carpets.

We took him in for surgery. The surgery itself was successful. But as the surgeons prepared him for anaesthesia, Brick had another seizure. It left him with a hind leg that collapsed unpredictably. He fell getting out of the way as Joan backed her car out of the garage. That already weakened leg suffered one broken bone and some torn muscles.

He spent the next days learning to lurch around on three legs. He did not once let out a whimper of self-pity. He was not short-tempered. He never snapped at us. And despite his obvious pain and difficulty moving, he never once forgot he was housebroken.

Because he was too wobbly to struggle up and down stairs, I built a ramp for him off our deck. Usually, he avoided crossing planks and narrow bridges. But he learned to use his ramp. On his own.

Most people (including me) lament lost opportunities, lost youth, lost earning power… If Brick had such thoughts, he didn't show them. He simply accepted his new situation.

*A dog has the soul of a philosopher.*
— PLATO

Dag Hammarskjöld, former Secretary-General of the United Nations, summarized his faith in this short prayer: "For all that has been, thanks. For all that will be, yes." Even in his dying, Brick lived that philosophy. I wish I could do it as well as he did.

36

*The wind flew. God told to wind to condense itself and out of the flurry came the horse. But with the spark of spirit the horse flew by the wind itself.*

— Marguerite Henry, *King of the Wind*

# 3

# In Their Own Right

PETS ARE MORE THAN JUST THE PROPERTY OF THEIR OWNERS

A flock of geese went overhead one afternoon, heading south – that classic V-shape of dark birds silhouetted against the sky, wings beating rhythmically... But there was something strange about them: they weren't honking.

Apparently no one knows for sure why geese honk as they fly. It seems to serve no useful purpose. Indeed, it must consume energy that they could better use for flying. But still, geese honk.

I remember being in Hazelton, one March, in northern B.C. The trees were still bare; late snow still littered last fall's leaves; scarcely a sound broke the lingering grip of winter. Then, distantly, we heard something. And over the looming hulk of Rocher de Boule Mountain came a massive flight of geese, several hundred of them, darkening the sky the way passenger pigeons used to, heading farther north. The sound stirred my heart, awakening primeval passions I hadn't known were there.

So when I see geese flying without any sound at all, I wonder what's wrong. Do they know something I don't? Of course they do. They know how to fly. And how to navigate long distances without maps or GPS monitors.

*Be like the bird that, pausing in her flight awhile on boughs too slight, feels them give way beneath her, and yet sings, knowing that she hath wings.*

– VICTOR HUGO, FRENCH NOVELIST AND POET

39

We humans arrogantly picture ourselves as the pinnacle of creation, the only beings capable of communication, abstract thought, writing, technology… From that flimsy self-assessment (in which we clearly have a conflict of interest) we conclude that other creatures are not capable of rational thought, of emotions, of learning.

Yet no human pilot could land on a swaying twig in a gusty wind and stay upright. No human technology can detect drugs or scents as well as a dog's nose. Humans have yet to develop a fibre proportionately as strong as a spider's silk.

The problem, I suspect, is that we keep asking the wrong questions. We persist in thinking of animals as imperfect imitations of ourselves – just as, for so many years, we thought of children as adults-in-training. We should evaluate animals in their own context.

A heron surged out of the trees along the lakeshore one day, as I was walking my dog. It swooped low over the water, long trailing legs almost surfing the surface, wings spread with not a feather twitching. At the last second, it pulled up and landed on a weathered piling. A heron on land is a somewhat gawky and ungainly creature. A heron in the air is effortless beauty.

In Africa, a couple of years ago, we saw marabou storks, usually standing around a waterhole. The guidebook described them as "enormous *ugly* birds [the guidebook's emphasis] whose long white legs are usually covered with its own excrement." We concurred with that description – on land. But in the air…

I watched one marabou stork glide in to land in a thicket of acacia trees near me. It had a wingspan of close to eight feet, yet it came banking through the branches with a grace and precision that took my breath away.

Watching birds on dry land does them an injustice. They need to be seen in their element – the air – to be fully appreciated.

Even the flightless penguin, a clown on its feet, flies superbly in the water.

## THE ELEMENT OF RELATIONSHIPS

Every creature has its natural element. We move inefficiently in water – although fins and air tanks help us considerably. Unassisted by technology, we fly about as well as a rock. Even on land, we humans are less graceful than a cheetah, less agile than a monkey, less powerful than a horse…

But are land, water, and air the only elements? Perhaps they're only the most obvious elements. Could relationships be an element?

When I was a lot younger, I thought the ultimate ideal was to be independent, to be self-sufficient, to owe nothing to anyone and to be owed nothing by anyone. As I grow older, I sense that such a person is not a human at all, but a caricature, a cardboard cut-out, a dysfunctional figment of cultural misanthropy.

More and more, I believe that we become fully human only in our relationships. All creatures have some sort of family or tribal function.

*The reason birds can fly and we can't is simply that they have perfect faith, for to have faith is to have wings.*

– JAMES MATTHEW BARRIE, AUTHOR *PETER PAN*

41

> *Dogs love their friends and bite their enemies, quite unlike people, who are incapable of pure love and always have to mix love and hate.*
>
> — SIGMUND FREUD

Only humans add the overlapping layers of politics, science, employment, recreation… We are not conscious of this element, just as I'm sure fish are not conscious of the water they swim in. But without relationships, we humans are as lost as a fish out of water.

And I think that animals are often better at relationships than we humans are. Our dog Phoebe believes that all human beings are kind, generous, and would just love to pat her head and rub her long, silky ears.

In general, I think she's right. Sure, there are some rotten apples in any barrel – hustlers, pimps, frauds… In the animal world, they might be the predators – wolves, tigers, sharks. Or the carrion-eaters – vultures, buzzards, hyenas. Typically, they prey on the weakest and most vulnerable in society – the bewildered elderly, the impressionable young, the mentally challenged. But they're a minority. I have met very few people who don't respond warmly and compassionately to others, face to face.

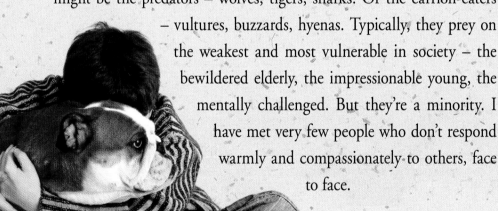

## Communicating Emotions

For several generations, the general pattern has been to deny that animals have feelings. We don't care how cattle feel, herded through chutes at meat processing plants. Horse trainers try to break the spirit of a horse. Dog owners beat their dogs. Scientists conduct experiments which prove – at least to their satisfaction – that animals do not feel pain as we do, do not think as we do, do not communicate as we do…

Yet every pet owner knows, beyond any doubt, that their pets have feelings. And pets can, in non-verbal ways, communicate those feelings.

Our dog Brick knew instantly that when suitcases came out, some kind of a change was coming. He lay at the head of the stairs, where we had to step over him every time we took something down to the car. He watched everything we did with brimming eyes.

His emotions were even more evident when we returned to pick him up at the boarding kennels. On one of these occasions, I heard Brick in the corridor long before he burst into the waiting room. Seeing us, he yelped, howled, groaned, growled, and whimpered all at once. He spun around so fast that his feet couldn't hold him up anymore; he collapsed to the floor, still thrashing.

There was a sad-eyed Doberman in the waiting room, limping around with one bandaged paw, soaking up sympathy. The Doberman eyed all this excitement with disdain, and backed cautiously into a corner, well out of the way of Brick's flailing paws.

*Who can believe that there is no soul behind those luminous eyes!*

– THEOPHILE GAUTIER, FRENCH POET

A less expressive dog, that Doberman. More like most humans. We're suspicious of letting our feelings overflow. So we choke back our tears in sorrow and restrain our exuberance in joy.

Pets like Brick have something to teach us. When we're happy, when we're grateful for the way life has dealt us our cards, we should show it. Exuberantly.

The danger, of course, is what's commonly called "anthropomorphizing." That is, attributing human emotions to creatures – or things – that aren't supposed to have those feelings. Walt Disney Pictures does it constantly. Bambi was never really a deer, but a human who looked like a deer. The same with the Lion King and his friends.

In her book *Animals in Translation*, Temple Grandin argues that animal emotions are more than just a reaction to current events. They are actually a technique to prepare for the future. The antelope who doesn't feel fear will not keep a watchful eye out for the lioness stalking her. The foolhardy mouse who ventures into open spaces will soon make a meal for a cat or an owl.

"We humans tend to think of emotions as dangerous forces that need to be strictly controlled by reason and logic," Grandin writes. "But that's not how the brain works. In the brain, logic and reason are never separate from emotion…You *feel like* you're using logic, but you're actually using logic guided by emotion. You just aren't aware of the emotion."

*Purring would seem to be, in her case, an automatic safety valve device for dealing with happiness overflow.*

– MONICA EDWARDS, AUTHOR

45

Grandin argues that animals are far more intelligent than we give them credit for being. Most of the intelligence tests we devise for animals, for example, don't test their intelligence at all. They merely test their ability to obey our commands.

Do we really prove anything about dolphin intelligence by teaching them to leap through a hoop? How much better do we understand seals because we can train them to balance a ball on their nose? Or pigeons because we can train them to peck at a light bulb to get food?

Sometimes children recognize that flaw in reasoning better than adults do. I trained our first dog, the terrier named Mickey, to turn somersaults. Most dogs "roll over" from one side to the other. Mickey tucked his head between his front legs, went tail over teakettle and came up standing. He could also beg, and walk a few steps on his hind legs.

Proudly, I made Mickey demonstrate his abilities to a boy visiting us. "Pooh," he scoffed. "Those are all people tricks. Can't he do any dog tricks?"

Grandin suggests that if we really want to determine animal intelligence, we need to look at what animals are able to teach themselves.

Migratory birds, for example, learn their routes from a single exposure to that terrain. Those routes are not hard-wired into their DNA. It's commonly taken for granted that birds – and Monarch butterflies

*Pet lovers know that animals sometimes understand us better than we do.*

— TONY SNOW, BROADCASTER, COLUMNIST

46

– instinctively know how to migrate. They don't. They have to learn that route from flying it with other members of their species.

An Ontario man named Bill Lishman proved that. Some local people had been trying to save endangered whooping cranes by raising them in captivity, but it wasn't working. Temple Grandin writes:

> When the babies were brought up without any migrating adults
> to teach them the routes, there was no way to re-introduce them
> to the wild. They didn't know how to migrate, so when winter
> came they would just stay put and die in the cold.

Bill Lishman had the idea of teaching the whooping cranes to migrate by leading them along the migration path in his ultralight plane… He started out working with Canada geese, because geese aren't in any danger of going extinct… Mr. Lishman managed to show that you could teach geese to follow a human in an ultralight airplane, *and* you could teach them a 400-mile one-way migration route flying it just once. No human being could memorize a 400-mile route across unmarked open terrain after travelling it just once. But bird migration is an extreme talent.

After he knew he could do it with geese, he switched to sandhill cranes, which are related to whooping cranes… In 1997 he led seven sandhill cranes from southern Ontario down to Virginia… The cranes spent the winter in Virginia, and then, one day at the end of March, they went out for their daily foraging and didn't come back. Two days later, Mr. Lishman got a call from a school principal in Ontario who said he had six big birds in his schoolyard entertaining the students! Six of the seven birds had made it the whole 400 miles back to Canada, after having flown the route only once in their lives, and in the opposite direction.

Even more remarkable is the achievement of a parrot named Alex, who has apparently reached the mental level of a four- or five-year-old human. I can't tell the story better than Grandin:

One day the corporate sponsors…wanted to show off what Alex could do. So they put a bunch of colored plastic refrigerator letters on a tray and started asking Alex questions.

"Alex, what sound is blue?"

Alex made the sound "Sssss." That was right.

Dr. Pepperberg said, "Good birdie," and Alex said, "Want a nut," because he was supposed to get a nut whenever he gave the right answer.

But Dr. Pepperberg didn't want him sitting there eating a nut during the limited time she had with their sponsors, so she told Alex to wait, and then asked, "What sound is green?"

The green example was the letter combination "SH" and Alex said "Ssshh." He was right again.

Dr. Pepperberg said, "Good parrot," and Alex said, "Want a nut."

But Dr. Pepperberg said, "Alex, wait. What sound is orange?"

Alex got that one right too, and he *still* didn't get his nut. They just kept going on and on… Alex was getting more frustrated by the minute.

Finally, Alex lost his patience. Here's the way Dr. Pepperberg describes it. Alex "gets very slitty-eyed and he looks at me and states, 'Want a nut. Nnn, uh, tuh.'"

Alex had spelled "nut."

# EXAMPLES OF INTELLIGENCE

It seems to me, as I read these examples, that we humans have vastly underestimated the intelligence of animals in general. Pet owners, of course, need no research to believe in their particular pet's intelligence. I couldn't count the number of people who have told me that their bug-eyed chihuahua "understands every word I say."

Sceptics cite the case of Clever Hans, a German horse who was supposed to be able to count. Hans's owner, William van Osten, asked his horse to add, say, 7 and 5, and Hans would tap 12 times with his hoof. Apparently, he could even tap out answers to questions like, "If the eighth day of the month comes on Tuesday, what is the date for the following Friday?"

Eventually, critics showed that Hans wasn't really counting. He was responding to tiny, unconscious cues from his human questioner.

But the critics' denial of Hans's intelligence reveals their own bias. Because Hans proved, in fact, that he could detect – and understand – cues so subtle, so invisible, that his human questioners were totally unaware of them.

Not only that, Hans taught himself to recognize those cues. Nobody taught those commands to the horse, because no one was aware of giving them. This was a horse teaching itself. That's the kind of intelligence we need to acknowledge.

And to celebrate.

*Like human beings, horses are all individuals with singular personalities, their own virtues and their own faults. We become bound to them for their beauty, their eccentricities, their heart and the love they so often return to us.*

— LANA SLATON

If animals have emotions, and if they have intelligence, then we also have to wonder whether they have their own awareness of God, something I will explore in the next chapter. This perception raises a question: How should we treat animals?

The image that comes into my mind is of a breakfast I shared with friends. Mike Schwartzentruber and I joined Bev and Ralph Milton on their back porch one summer morning, soon after Mike and I had both moved out west from Toronto.

Bev and Ralph had a hummingbird feeder hung from the eaves for weeks, without attracting any hummingbirds. That morning, we sat around the patio table eating breakfast and chattering animatedly. Suddenly, I could sense something throbbing above me, as if the air itself were vibrating. Mike had been talking; his voice faded away into silence.

Slowly, so slowly, I twisted around so that I could watch the tiny, bright-feathered bird hovering almost over my head. Its wings moved so fast that they were literally invisible, though it was little more than an arm's length away. I could see the wing roots, though, and its tiny pectoral muscles working away; its feet, smaller than a fingernail clipping, tucked up tight under its belly; its tail hooking down sometimes to control its balance. It was so fragile, so delicate…

It sipped the sweet nectar from the feeder. And then it was gone.

We all sighed, simultaneously.

"I think," Mike breathed, "that I have just seen a miracle."

*Spirituality is like a bird. If you hold it too closely, it chokes. And if you hold it too loosely, it escapes.*

– Israel Salanter Lipkin

*The fish in the water is silent, the animal on the earth is noisy, the bird in the air is singing. But man has in him the silence of the sea, the noise of the earth and the music of the air.*

RABINDRANATH TAGORE, INDIAN POET

# 4
# Deepest Yearnings

DO PETS HAVE SOULS? DOES IT MATTER?

A family of squirrels had set up house in an old cottonwood whose core had rotted out. Then a car ran over the mother, and orphaned the three little kits. The baby squirrels survived only because a woman who lived nearby started bringing them peanuts and raisins and bits of fruit.

Still, squirrels have fairly short life expectancies. I thought only one of them had survived the next winter to reach adulthood. When I walked my dog Brick, I usually stopped by the old cottonwood. The squirrel would come out onto a branch and have a little chat with me, while Brick went squirrelly down below, trying to climb the tree to get at it.

Then, one autumn day, the squirrel didn't come out. I found a small furry carcass lying in the weeds. It was a squirrel. "Our" squirrel, I feared. I expected Brick to grab the carcass as if he had finally caught his tormenter. Instead, he gave the dead body only a cursory sniff before trotting on.

On the other hand, he still kept trying to climb the old, hollow cottonwood. "Don't bother," I told him. "There's no squirrel there any-more. It's dead." But he knew better than I did. Because a few days

later, I saw "our" squirrel perched on a branch, its tail curled up along its back, its rodent teeth gnawing away on a pine cone.

I still wonder how Brick knew the difference between the dead squirrel and the live one. I suppose each squirrel has its own unique scent, but there must be something more to it.

Brick was a bird dog, genetically engineered to chase birds. A sparrow on our feeder, a pheasant strolling through the yard, a duck paddling in the lake would kick those genes into overdrive. But he would show no interest at all in a dead bird – not even one that died moments before, trying to fly through a window. One quick snuffle to check it out, and he would turn away.

Does life itself have a smell? Does something definable leave a body at the moment of death?

## DEFINING THE SOUL

Some years back, a medical researcher claimed to have detected the human soul empirically. He took precise measurements of patient weights. If I recall his research correctly, he found that immediately after death, patients weighed 21 grams less. That, he decided, was the weight of the human soul, leaving its human body.

I was sceptical. I still am.

For me, the soul is a mystery. I don't believe it can be tested, measured, or captured. But Brick clearly recognized a difference between alive and dead.

I remember a story about a boy who found a bird lying in the road. He brought it home to his mother.

"Oh, too bad," she said, "the little bird is dead."

"Then why hasn't it gone to heaven?" the boy asked.

"It's a bit hard to explain," she said at last. "Part of it has gone to heaven."

"I know, Mommy," said her son. "It's the part that sings."

They made a small hole in the ground, and buried the dead bird in it. But only the part that was left behind.

If there's a soul, "the part that sings" makes a pretty good definition. Or the part that purrs. Or barks. Or loves.

*Look at the birds*
*flying around:*
*they do not plant seeds,*
*gather a harvest and put*
*it in barns;*
*yet your Father*
*in heaven takes care*
*of them!*

– MATTHEW 6:26A, GOOD NEWS BIBLE

57

The really great thing about
cats is their endless variety.
One can pick a cat to fit
almost any kind of decor,
colour, scheme, income,
personality, mood.
But under the fur, whatever
the colour it may be,
there still lies, essentially
unchanged, one of the world's
free souls.

— ERIC GURNEY, CARTOONIST

# Beyond Our Imagining

Joan and I saw our neighbour Del Schlosser driving his truck very slowly down his driveway to the end of their property, where a thicket of wild rose bushes grew in a gully. He had something brown and furry lying across the tailgate of his truck.

"It must be Cola," said Joan.

Cola was Del's lovable 13-year-old elkhound. Ever since we moved here, I could count on Cola coming around to our house every morning, tail wagging, head lowered so I could rub her ears.

But that morning, she hadn't come around.

I got up to go and give Del a hand.

Joan looked doubtful. "He may just want to be alone," she reminded me.

I knew that Del wouldn't want to talk about it. But I figured he might not mind a helping shovel. Men don't share their feelings much. Men work together. But as they work together, in a word here and a phrase there, they do say what needs to be said. And so, as our shovels grated in the earth, Del told me – in bits and pieces – how it happened.

"I went into the garage," he said, "and she didn't come trotting up. So I looked on the other side of the car. She was just lying there. No pain, no fuss. She just died."

It took longer than that to say, though, because Del had to keep turning away to clean his shovel.

*You think dogs will not be in heaven? I tell you, they will be there long before any of us.*

– Robert Louis Stevenson, NOVELIST

61

*If there are no dogs in Heaven, then when I die I want to go where they went.*

— WILL ROGERS, AMERICAN ENTERTAINER

Cola didn't fit perfectly into the pit we had dug for her. Gently, Del adjusted the position of her legs. She lay there on the bottom as if she were still sleeping.

When we started shovelling earth back into the pit, we both instinctively avoided her face. We cringed at the thought of sand getting into her nostrils, into her mouth, into her eyes… So first we shovelled sand onto her hind quarters. Then onto her chest. When we couldn't stall any longer, Del leaned down and stroked Cola's cheek one last time. He made sure her eyes were closed.

Then, and only then, he gently slid a shovel of sand over her face.

We knew that Cola no longer lived in the body we had just buried. Yet we were not capable of imagining her any other way.

Our minds, our experience, tell us that when a person – or a pet – dies, that's it. There is no more. They're gone.

But our hearts won't believe it.

## A SENSE OF LOSS

Cynics might say that this is just a refusal to accept reality. A life has ended; that's all there is. The late rabbi Reuben Slonim told me, many times, that classical Judaism recognizes only this life. We have one chance to get it as right as fallible humans can, and then it's over.

But something deep inside us says that there must be more. And so a child draws a picture of his pet fish that died, and colours a halo over its head. Another child holds a burial service for a bird – for the part that doesn't sing anymore. Our son, Stephen, wept for days over the death of our cat Sylvester. He didn't cry as much over the death of his grandfather, my wife's father. As he explained, "I hardly knew Grandpa, but Sylvester was part of our family."

In our society, pets are often a child's first exposure to death. Generally, we shield the young from death. We spirit the sick and dying away to hospital wards or nursing homes; the sicker and weaker they get, the less likely we are to take small children to visit them.

But pets live and die at home. Especially pets with shorter lives, like hamsters and fish. But also cats. Our children saw Sylvester when he was only hours old, because Tuppence chose to have her kittens on our bed, in the middle of the night. When the kids got up in the morning, they saw six tiny, mewling kittens crawling all over each other to get at their mother's milk. Just five years later, they saw Sylvester's coat lose its shine, his eyes lose their brightness, his body lose its energy.

And when he died, they cried. For his loss, and for theirs. Because he was "part of our family."

And perhaps that's the important thing — not whether we can prove the existence of a soul, but whether we can believe in it. Because if we believe in it, we will treat our pets, our friends, and the whole created order in a different way. They can no longer merely be things, objects, to be used for our benefit and then discarded, alive or dead. If they have souls, they have a relationship with God – just like us.

I remember the time Joan and I sat down to have lunch at our picnic table outside. Brick cantered up to the table, plunked his jowls on the edge of it, and stared at our sandwiches. If telekinesis worked, those sandwiches should have voluntarily slid across the table into his mouth.

With my eyes dutifully closed, I started to say grace. "For this food, dear God –"

Someone burped. A rich, rolling, resonant "Burrrrrrupppp!"

It was the dog.

Joan dissolved in hysterical laughter. I tried desperately to keep a straight face.

"That probably expresses gratitude better than anything I could say," I rationalized.

Whether a burp is an acceptable grace depends on your understanding of prayer. If you expect prayer to use familiar words and phrases, it won't be. When I was a small child, my bedtime prayers followed a unchanging ritual that always concluded with the same sequence: "God bless Grandpa and Grandma in Canada, and Granny and Grandpa in Ireland, and God bless Mommy and Daddy, and make me a good boy. Amen."

Over the years, I've grown less and less comfortable with memorized formulas. They trip too easily off the tongue. One phrase follows another, like beads on a string.

A few years ago, I caught the last bits of an interview on radio. Almost as an afterthought, the interviewer asked, "What is prayer?"

The interviewee replied, "Prayer is the deepest longing of the heart."

I loved that definition. Because that kind of prayer doesn't need words. What someone really longs for, hungers and thirsts for, will shape every aspect of that person's life. It will reach out in that person's actions and relationships. And that person's words.

So if Brick's burp expressed his deepest longing, it was indeed a prayer.

*If having a soul means being able to feel love and loyalty and gratitude, then animals are better off than a lot of humans.*

— James Herriot, scottish veterinarian and writer

*I care not for a man's religion whose dog and cat are not the better for it.*

– ABRAHAM LINCOLN

*For each is born with such a throat as thanks his God with every note.*

– JUDITH WRIGHT, *MAGPIES*

66

Maybe that's wishful thinking. Maybe we simply hope that our animal friends have a relationship with God in their own right. But if it's just wishful thinking, it seems to be an idea that's growing in popularity.

As evidence, I offer the growing number of services for the blessing of animals. My own churches, the ones I have belonged to, have never held such a service. But neighbouring churches – Anglican and Lutheran, mostly – have. And members of my churches have taken their dogs and cats, their snakes and budgies and gerbils, to those services. Clearly the ritual of blessing means something to those pet owners.

And perhaps even to the pets – although we should never assume that a worship service designed for human understandings should also appeal to animal sensibilities. Nevertheless, as one participant told me later, "It was amazing how well behaved they all were. It was almost as if they understood something important was happening."

David Butler-Jones, the Public Health Officer for Canada, told me once about visiting a remote lake on a canoe trip in northern Ontario.

"Usually," he said, "you see loons alone, or in pairs. But one time, on a canoe trip, we saw at least a dozen loons, gathered in a circle, with their young ones in the middle. They were all facing each other. Every now and then, one of them would rise higher in the water, and call, and the others responded.

"I don't know what they were doing. But it was obviously important to them, whatever it was."

To David, it looked uncommonly like an act of corporate worship.

When Brick went for his morning walk, he bolted through the front door, and then came to a complete stop. Nothing moved except his nose. Even his eyes closed.

Maybe he was just sniffing to see who had been around during the night. But his actions resemble my own reactions when I step into the stained glass splendour of a medieval cathedral. I try to absorb the cool, the hush, the multi-hued magnificence. I take a deep breath, soaking in the glory that all those people, all those years ago, dedicated to God.

I've had the same feeling in what Celtic Christians called "thin spaces," those special places where the usual gulf between human and divine shrinks.

Can we really imagine that our pets can worship God? Many people before us have believed they could. Traditions around the Christmas story have the domestic animals gathering around the manger and kneeling. Poet Thomas Hardy exploited that tradition in "The Oxen":

> We pictured the meek mild creatures where
> They dwelt in their strawy pen,
> Nor did it occur to one of us there
> To doubt they were kneeling then...

In fact, many of us still sing about it in familiar Christmas carols:

> Ox and ass before him bow
> And He is in the manger now...

I don't offer those quotations as proof that animals have souls – I offer them only as evidence that we want to believe they do. I don't expect that anyone will prove that animals do, or do not, have their own direct relationship with the divine – at least, not in my lifetime. But our own attitudes are crucial.

Relationships are, at root, emotional. For a century or more, a certain segment of society has argued that animals do have emotions as we do, simply because there is no way of measuring those emotions. All scientists can do is observe certain behaviour patterns, but these prove nothing. Exactly the same could be said of humans. There is no way to measure our degree of pain, or joy, or love. All anyone can do is observe certain behaviour patterns.

If we treat our pets – and all animals – as if they, too, are capable of having a personal relationship with the divine, however that may happen, then we cannot treat them merely as things. In the terms popularized by theologian and philosopher Martin Buber, a century ago, our connection to them has to be more "I-thou" than "I-it."

Our pets may not be human. But neither are they objects, to be used or abused at our pleasure.

They matter to God. Therefore they should also matter to us.

*Horses change lives. They give our young people confidence and self-esteem.*
*They provide peace and tranquility to troubled souls — they give us hope!*

— TONI ROBINSON

# 5

# Making Connections with Scripture

HISTORIC RELIGIOUS UNDERSTANDINGS EMERGE INTO NEW LIGHT

Our cat Tuppence developed arthritis around the age of 12. She couldn't jump as high as she used to. But she still liked to get up into the bathroom window – the highest point in the house – where she could peer out and survey her front yard.

One morning, while I was washing my face at the sink, Tuppence stood by my feet and yowled. I pushed the clutter to the back of the counter, so that she could jump up onto it safely, and from there to the window.

Still she yowled.

"Go ahead and jump," I spluttered through the lather. "The counter's clear."

"Meeiiaaaooooww!" she replied.

"Quit complaining and jump," I told her. "You know you can do it."

"Yiaaaoooww…"

"Look cat, I've got things of my own to do. I am not going to lift you!"

"Iiaooooww…"

In the end, of course, I did lift her. I scooped her up, and placed her safely over my head in the window.

"Merrmp!" she grunted, in what I took to be a thank you.

As I stood there, it occurred to me that I had acted out a Bible story. That incident with Tuppence was almost a replica of several stories that Jesus told. He talked about people knocking on doors in the middle of the night, until finally the frustrated owner opened up and offered help. He referred to children bugging their parents to get fed. He told about a woman who pestered a judge until she got a fair hearing. And though they didn't want to, the people hiding behind their locked doors or their authority eventually gave up trying to ignore the intrusions, and yielded. Just the way I eventually yielded and lifted my cat.

*Cats seem to go on the principle that it never does any harm to ask for what you want.*

– JOSEPH WOOD KRUTCH, NATURE WRITER

72

## HANDED OVER

In my Christian tradition, the Bible is central. I have learned a lot about the Bible from my pets. I suspect the same would be true of any other religion's scriptures, if people could break free from the mindset that they can only learn from texts and teachers.

Of course, pets can't read. And they can't talk. Or write. Which means they can't possibly teach us the way we usually expect to be taught. They can't tell us what they think we should know. It's up to us to make the connections.

Tuppence continued to give me insights about the Bible right to the end of her life. I had read a book which spent pages showing that the biblical words we usually read as "betrayed" really meant "handed over" in the original Greek. I didn't get the point – until I "handed over" Tuppence to the vet.

*Cats are intended to teach us that not everything in nature has a purpose.*

– GARRISON KEILLOR,
AUTHOR, RADIO BROADCASTER

*The smallest feline is a masterpiece.*

– LEONARDO DA VINCI

Tuppence was almost 20. She probably should have died years before. She had lost battles with cars, hockey nets, Dobermans, and countless neighbouring cats. Her hind legs didn't always do what she wanted them to do anymore; nor did her kidneys. She slept 23 hours a day. She was stone deaf, with a cataract in one eye, and only one canine tooth left.

But she was still part of our family.

One day, one of her remaining teeth abscessed. Her cheek puffed out as if she had a marble tucked into the corner of her mouth.

"Surgery?" I asked our veterinarian.

The vet nodded. "She hasn't the strength to withstand the infection without it."

Together, we considered the alternatives. Tuppence would die without surgery. She might die during surgery. Even if she survived, whatever life she had left would be shortened by the surgery's after-effects.

I picked Tuppence up one last time, and stroked her head. She purred. It broke my heart. She lay in my arms, and she purred.

With a sick feeling, I handed Tuppence over to the vet.

In that instant, I understood the theologian's point. You can be let down by someone, even betrayed, and still have some hope, some control over your own destiny. But for Tuppence, being "handed over" – even to the kindest and most gentle of veterinarians – was the end. And we all knew it.

For Jesus, being "handed over" to the local authorities – who were anything but kind and gentle – was also the end. And everyone knew it.

## During "The Dark Night of the Soul"

Over and over, when I find the long-ago culture of the Bible baffling, pets have given me clues.

The Hebrew prophet Isaiah, for example, wrote to a people who had been exiled and enslaved in Babylon; they had felt abandoned by God. Isaiah portrayed God as a husband who has temporarily forsaken a young wife, cast her off, and hidden his face from her in anger. Then "with compassion" the husband takes the wife back again.

At first, I didn't like what the text seemed to be saying. I object to macho males who abandon their wives, have their fling, and then expect the wives to welcome them back. That's what it sounded like. It may have been a meaningful analogy in Isaiah's time, but in my time I felt it an offensive description for God. I don't want to worship a fickle, self-indulgent, perpetual adolescent!

But then I remembered our first dog. Mickey was just a mutt – a happy, yappy, brown-and-white terrier. We found him in the dog pound. Something bright in Mickey's eyes, something in the way he cocked his ears and puckered his brow, attracted us. We paid our fee and took him home.

The first evening we had him, we had to go out and leave him alone. I can still see his look of sorrow, of bewilderment, as we closed the front door and left him inside.

And I will never, ever, forget the welcome he gave us when we returned. He didn't merely wag his tail. He wagged everything. He vibrated himself into such ecstasy that his paws barely touched the floor.

Through the years we had him, he always greeted us with the same exuberance. The overflowing joy of his welcome helped heal the pain of temporary separation.

Mickey never understood why we had to leave him alone sometimes, any more than we can understand why God seems absent in times of depression or turmoil, or when violence and injustice engulf the world. But while we were absent, he guarded our property. And he waited patiently for us.

Mickey showed me what to do during those times someone called "the dark night of the soul." Look after God's concerns. Be faithful. Believe that God still cares and will return. And whenever God is present, live in overflowing joy.

## A Different Culture

You won't get these insights by looking for stories about pets in any sacred scriptures. Those stories come out of a time and a culture that didn't have pets as we know them. They had domestic animals – cattle and sheep, dogs and cats, perhaps birds – because humans seem hard-wired to collect creatures. When I was a boy, attending a school in northern India, we often made pets out of the giant beetles found in the Himalayan foothills, even though we never got any indication they might reciprocate our affection.

Most of the world still doesn't have pets the way we do in North America and Europe. An acquaintance from Tobago, in the Caribbean, observed the lavish treatment given our pets – special food, special beds, day care, pet sitters, baths, grooming… He commented, wryly, "If there is an afterlife, I want to come back as a Canadian dog!"

The Bible doesn't have much to say about dogs – and what it does say isn't very complimentary. But in one stunning passage, Jesus tells a Canaanite/Phoenician woman that he came to teach his own Jewish people, not Gentiles like her. He described her people as "dogs."

She replied, bravely, "Even the dogs at the table get some scraps."

And Jesus changed his mind, and healed her daughter.

The passage suggests to me that Jesus must have felt compassion for animals, as well as for children. The woman's comment touched his heart in some way.

Poverty limits the ability of most of the world's people to treat pets as we do. Through much of Asia, cats consider themselves lucky to escape the soup pot. In Thailand, un-neutered dogs have crossbred themselves into a uniform mutt, in various shades of brown, about the size and shape of a short-haired terrier, that roams the streets living on garbage.

# Not an Easy Life

Most of the year, our yard is a riot of birds. In winter, they gobble up the seeds we put out for them; in summer they feast on the bugs that hold their annual convention in Joan's roses.

When Jesus talked about the lilies of the field and the birds of the air, we think of them leading an idyllic life. They have no worries, no cares. God provides for them.

But there's another side to their existence.

Sparrows had so little value in biblical times that they were sold two for a penny. Their lives still aren't worth very much. A sudden cold snap in winter freezes them by the thousands. Even in summer, they're constantly searching for food. They don't have time to watch a sunset or smell the roses. But then, if I had to eat my weight in seeds – or bugs – every day, I probably wouldn't have much free time either. I'd flap around even more frantically than the average sparrow. Birds work a lot harder for their daily bread than we do.

Plants can't chase food the way birds do, but that doesn't make their lives any easier. One weekend, I forgot to water our hanging baskets. Saturday morning, a small fuchsia was a fountain of bright red flowers; by Sunday afternoon, it was a withered corpse. Jesus acknowledged that plants could blossom one day and scorch the next.

Birds and plants don't necessarily have a life to be envied. They have one advantage over us, though. They're never tempted to think that they achieve their survival by their own efforts.

*Aren't five sparrows sold for two pennies? Yet not one sparrow is forgotten by God.*

– LUKE 12:6, GOOD NEWS BIBLE

One time, a big black-and-white tomcat paused outside our basement windows to spray his mark on window frames and shrubs. Our cat Mush leaped onto the window ledge, hissing and spitting ferociously behind the safety of the glass.

I went outside and chased the strange cat away. When I came back in, Mush was strutting and preening along the top of the bookcases, as proud as if she had vanquished the foe herself.

In Mush, I can see the misplaced ego of the Exodus people, confident they had carved a place for themselves among the Canaanites by their own military prowess. I can see the vanity of some Pharisees of Jesus' time, confident that they had earned God's favour by strict adherence to the rules of their faith tradition.

I'm sure that's why so many newspaper comic strips – from Peanuts to Garfield – focus on children and pets. Instead of getting defensive, we smile ruefully when we see our foibles and failings exposed in the behaviour of creatures who are, to our adult minds, slightly lower in the hierarchy of God's favourites.

*To err is human,*
*to purr, feline*

– Robert Byrne

## A Different Perspective

The holy scriptures of all faiths were written by a privileged elite – mostly male, usually priests and military or political leaders. I wonder, sometimes, how different those scriptures might have been, if written from a perspective lower down the religious totem pole.

Our dog Phoebe disturbed a family of ducks. They exploded into the lake, beating the water into a froth to get away from this presumed predator. In the world of Irish setters, Phoebe is vocationally challenged. She has no interest in birds. She doesn't even know how to swim. But the mother duck doesn't know that. So although the small ones were well out from the shore, the mother duck still thrashed back and forth just beyond the dog's nose, quacking furiously. "Chase *me*!" the duck seemed to be saying. "Leave my little ones alone!"

I've seen similar behaviour from other mothers. Ptarmigan and quail will feign a broken wing to lure predators away from their chicks. Even crocodiles, not known for sentimental feelings, show occasional maternal instincts.

In Jasper National Park, families of wild goats graze on public lawns. One of the youngsters got curious about me as I took pictures. Maybe my beard reminded it of its father. It cocked its head to one side. Then it came toddling towards me. Its mother, until then, had been paying more attention to the grass than to her offspring. Her golden eyes had a faraway glaze; she munched methodically, mindlessly. But when her lamb trotted towards me, suddenly, she was all eyes. And horns. And sharp little hooves doing a kind of tap dance. I backed away quickly. To be frank, I was scared of her.

When I read Mary's famous song in the gospel of Luke, tradition-ally called the *Magnificat*, I sense a mother's awareness of the potential dangers awaiting her unborn child, a tension about the kind of world her baby would be entering. Despite her youth, her lack of child-rearing

experience, the realization that she was carrying a new life sharpened her perceptions of the world around her. She saw with sudden clarity the injustices, the inequalities, the repression, of a world that until then she took for granted.

By my reading, the *Magnificat* is not so much about God's priorities as about a mother's. In her world, in that part over which she had any control, she was going to make sure that the rich and influential would not get better treatment than the poor and powerless. Those who needed food, or reassurance, or comfort would get it. Especially her child.

Her child would not have to look far to know what the kingdom of God was like.

So a mother duck makes me wonder how different the Bible might be, had its interpreters through the ages been mothers and children.

# 6
# Gateway to Justice

COMPASSION FOR ANIMALS ENCOURAGES BETTER TREATMENT FOR ALL

Four centuries ago, philosopher Rene Descartes offered his proof for human existence: "I think, therefore I am." We humans have applied his aphorism with a vengeance. Thinking – intellectual activity – became our Holy Grail. We defined ourselves by IQ tests. We turned worship into cerebral reflection. We constructed theological systems that depended on consistency and logic more than on any experience of God among us.

Worse, we allowed our idolatry of conscious thought to isolate us from each other, and from the rest of creation. Because animals don't think as we do – at least, they don't express their thoughts in words – we concluded that they must be a lesser order of creation. Therefore, we assumed, they don't suffer when punctured with birdshot; they don't scream when a harpoon drives into their necks; they don't go into shock when a bullet rips through their lungs...

Perhaps I'm anthropomorphizing – attributing human emotions to an animal. But that's all that I can do. I only have human emotions and experiences to work with. So the only way I can identify with any other creature is to consider first how I might feel in that situation.

*Folks will know how large your soul is, by the way you treat a dog!*

– CHARLES F. DORAN

## EMPATHY FOR ANIMALS

During the summer of 2003, newspapers across Canada carried a news item about a Quebec man who tried to kidnap a bear cub swimming in the Gatineau River, using his Jet Ski as a weapon. Canadian Press reported:

> The cub was swimming across the river…when Denis Ryan grabbed it. The bear broke free several times by clawing at Ryan and tried to swim to shore…
>
> To wear out the bear, Ryan ran over it with the Jet Ski, forcing the cub's head under water.
>
> The 55-year-old woodsman got his best grip on the cub by holding it upside down by one of its hind legs.
>
> He then dunked the animal repeatedly to drain the cub's energy.
>
> The cub was moaning, desperately trying to breathe…

*Mercy to animals means mercy to mankind.*

– Henry Bergh, founder, ASPCA

CP quotes Ryan as saying, "I kept dunking and kept dunking him…, I was never mean to the bear…"

I told that news story during a sermon the following Sunday. People came to me after the service, spluttering with outrage.

Thirty years ago, I wrote a magazine article about torture in Brazil, then in the grip of a military regime. One of the most common methods of torture was to dunk prisoners repeatedly. To hold them under water until they almost drowned, let them come up for just long enough to grab a breath, then dunk them again. If dunking is considered torture for humans, can it be anything less for animals?

Few Canadians have personal experience with torture, or oppression, or starvation. But they can recognize it, and get upset, when it involves animals. The local TV station knows that stories about maltreated animals – horses with their manes and tails matted with burrs, dogs with collars that have worn open wounds in their necks, starved cats locked inside a fetid house – will always evoke a massive public response.

Perhaps it goes back to childhood training, when we were taught by our parents to take care of our pets. To change the shavings in the gerbil cage. To keep water in the canary's drinking dish. To clean the kitty litter…

"Be gentle," our parents admonished us.

So when someone violates those long-held standards, we feel that our own values have been betrayed. In this way, our feelings towards our pets can raise our sensitivity to injustices and cruelty in the world.

*Whoever beats dogs loves not man.*

– ARSÈNE HOUSSAYE

## PETS AS GATEWAYS

*Respect and affection for animals, particularly those who share our homes, recognize no geographic borders.*

— NICK CLOONEY, BROADCASTER

Pets and other animals can act as a gateway. Our response to them can lead us towards either justice or injustice. I believe that as we learn compassion for our pets, we foster the habit of showing compassion to other creatures, including other humans.

One of Jesus' parables (in Eugene Peterson's contemporary translation, *The Message*) concludes with the maxim, "If you're a crook in small things, you'll be a crook in big things."

We all know that an investment counsellor who has been scrupu-
lously honest in small dealings will probably also be honest with big
money, and vice versa. A parent who snaps at children will probably
have a short fuse in business dealings. A driver who cuts corners on the
road may be tempted to cut corners in relationships.

The famous psychologist Carl Jung apparently described sentimen-
tality as "the mask of brutality." He must have been having a bad day.
I know that if I had to trust myself to someone else, I would far rather
choose someone who habitually showed kindness to animals than someone who habitually demonstrated cruelty.

Indeed, compassion for animals is a religious obligation for Islam,
Judaism, and Christianity. All three share a reverence for what Christians call the Old Testament of the Bible, which contains the story of
Noah. When a great flood wiped out all human life, according to that
story, Noah built a boat big enough to hold two of every kind of creature. When the flood receded, he returned those animals to dry land,
to repopulate the earth.

The book of Genesis says that God created the rainbow as a sign, a
"covenant," with Noah and his family "and with every living creature
that is with you." Not just once, but six times, God reminds Noah that
this agreement is "between me, and you, and every living creature…"
The repetition hammers home its point – human welfare and the welfare of nature are inextricably tied together.

*I love and respect all
animal life,
not just the traditionally
"cutesy" ones.*

– Jeff Vouladakis

89

*I really love pets. They're like children.*
*They know if you really love them or not.*
*You can't fool them.*

– DONNA DOUGLAS, ACTRESS

## RESPONSIBILITY, NOT DOMINION

The translators of the King James Version of the English Bible, in 1611, have a lot to answer for. In the first chapter, they stated that God gave humans "dominion...over all the earth..." The phrase implies that we can do what we want with the earth.

A more accurate translation, based on older texts than the King James translators had access to, might convey something more like "take responsibility for," "look after," or "put in charge of."

Instead, we have treated land, sea, and air as inexhaustible resources, to pillage for our own short-term gain. When John Cabot first sailed into Newfoundland waters in 1497, he reported that the cod were so thick they slowed the passage of his ship. In those days, seal populations burgeoned unchecked; that was long before anyone started culling seals to protect cod stocks. If an unlimited seal population didn't decimate cod stocks back then, I don't see how they can be blamed for doing it now. Overfishing nearly wiped out the cod. Not the seals. Left to itself, nature always seems to have enough.

Snorkelling in the British Virgin Islands, Joan and I swam into a miniature version of what Cabot's cod must have been like. Millions of minnows – like the guppies I once had in an aquarium, but bigger – hung in the water like a shimmering curtain.

At first, we avoided sudden motions, worried about frightening them away. Then we realized that a dozen ungainly pelicans, as black and awkward as pterodactyls, circled overhead. Periodically, they dived into

*People are not going to care about animal conservation unless they think animals are worthwhile.*

– DAVID ATTENBOROUGH, BROADCASTER, NATURALIST

the ocean in a tangle of wings and legs and gaping beaks. Immediately, they righted themselves, with little fish spilling out of the corners of their beaks. And gulped, long necks bobbing as they swallowed.

Below us, a huge grey ray – the same colour as a battleship and seemingly about as big – glared balefully at us for a moment, then slid away along the bottom, its wingtips undulating gracefully. Around the edges, in deeper water, a few kingfish prowled. But there were too many fish for them, too.

The rays, the pelicans, the kingfish – none of them would ever deplete the oceans of their food supplies. Even the pelicans eventually gave up feeding, and simply floated, letting the ocean support their bloated bellies.

Only we humans, using industrial-strength technologies, can wipe out the cod fishery on the Grand Banks, the salmon in the Pacific, and the buffalo on the prairies. The story of the Garden of Eden failed to anticipate the power of the Industrial Revolution. We humans would no longer be content with just one apple – we would strip the tree and then cut it down.

*Teach your children how to behave with animals.*

— SHELLY MORRISON, ACTRESS

*If people were superior to animals, they'd take better care of the world.*

— A. A. MILNE, AUTHOR

93

But there are signs of hope.

A friend lives in a 27 floor condominium complex in Ontario. The condominium complex's board of directors wanted to prohibit pets. The owners rebelled. Within their own private property, the owners insisted, they could do what they wanted. Including having pets.

The board didn't like pets. They decreed that no animals might touch any of the common property – the halls, elevators, lobby, laundry room, driveway, parking lot, and the interconnecting pipes and wires…

They thought that would take care of pets.

But the residents valued their animal friends enough to find a loophole in the laws. They carried cats or small dogs through the common areas. Those with bigger beasts used baby strollers, shopping carts, or wagons. When my friend's neighbour takes his large German Shepherd for a walk, the dog jumps obediently into a shopping cart. Panting excitedly, he rides the cart down in the elevator to the ground floor. At the edge of the condominium property, the dog leaps onto the ground and goes for his walk.

This kind of incident shows me that if animals matter enough to us, we can find ways around official – and sometimes officious – regulations. And so a growing number of people risk their bodies to block logging roads, to encircle endangered habitats of burrowing owls, or to volunteer for the SPCA.

## JUSTICE FOR ALL

About 20 years ago, I edited a book by Roman Catholic writer and priest James Conlon, called *Geo-Justice*. His thesis was fairly simple – it is not justice unless it is justice for the whole planet. Any attempt to serve one component of that planet without consideration of other components is short-sighted at best, harmful at worst. So it is not justice to assist the impoverished people of India or China to attain an American standard of living if that contributes to global warming and wipes out vulnerable frogs in swamps. But by the same token, it is not justice to deny development to poor humans to protect the frogs.

Justice must be justice for all. Including animals.

It seems like an impossible task. And then I remember the day a flock of Bohemian waxwings descended on our mountain ash tree. One minute, the tree was loaded with bright red berries; the next, it stood bare naked and shivering in the winter wind. Just as suddenly as they arrived, the waxwings lifted off en masse. They swirled around in the sky a couple of times, forming and re-forming like the constantly chang-

*Keep fighting for animals by making compassionate, cruelty-free choices every day and encouraging those around you to do the same.*

– BEA ARTHUR, ACTRESS

95

ing patterns in a kaleidoscope. First one bird was in front, then another. But they all wheeled and turned together as if they weren't 30 or 40 or 50 separate birds at all, but one, governed by a single collective mind.

One of my favourite biblical passages comes in Paul's letter to the Christian church at Philippi. "Let the same mind be in you," he wrote, "that was in Jesus Christ." Put in more colloquial terms, he was saying, "If Jesus is the model we emulate, then we should be so much like him that we even think like him."

I don't suggest that all members of a faith group should become identical little robots, mindlessly listening for instructions from their master's voice (like the RCA terrier seen on old vinyl record labels). But think of the impact that a group could have on society if the entire group acted quickly, decisively, and consistently.

Bishop Ron Rolheiser of Saskatchewan wrote a meditation in the *Prairie Messenger* newspaper. He suggested that one person's prayers didn't seem likely to alter the world. But, he suggested, suppose that one person organized an entire parish to pray for the same thing, and to live their prayer in their daily lives. That would have more impact. And then suppose that all the parishes and congregations in a national church were to coordinate their prayers, their lives, their commitments…

And then suppose that all the churches of an entire nation unified their efforts.

And then suppose that all two billion Christians around the world acted together…

If we could act as single-mindedly as those waxwings, and if we could extend to the entire world the compassion we feel for animals in general, and for our pets in particular, we might make a real difference to the world we live in.

# 7

# Angels in Fur and Feathers

THE HEALING AND THERAPEUTIC VALUE OF PETS

In a throwaway sentence in her book, *Animals in Translation*, Temple Grandin mused on how humans have changed horses and dogs by our association with them. But she wondered how dogs and horses might have changed us.

Our effect on domestic animals is perhaps most obvious among dogs. They have been bred, interbred, crossbred, purebred, and overbred until they come in every colour of the rainbow except green and in every size and shape from teacup to small bears.

We have similarly affected the shape and function of almost every other domestic animal – perhaps least successfully with cats. We now have horses as high-strung as violins, and horses with plodding hooves the size of pie pans. We have cows designed to give milk, and cows designed to give beef. We have mice specifically bred to be more susceptible to human diseases, and other mice specifically bred to be immune to those diseases.

*Therapy animals are widely employed in elder care to improve the quality of life.*

– WWW.ANIMALEDU.COM

*Animals are such agreeable friends — they ask no questions, they pass no criticisms.*

GEORGE ELIOT (MARY ANN EVANS), NOVELIST

But I've seen very little research into how animals have affected us. Yet it seems clear to me that they have, and they still do. Our animals – whether common or exotic – affect us by our relationship with them. In my search for stories to document this supposition, I found abundant evidence.

Sarah Schipman, for example, wrote an Internet article about Ann Vaincourt, an administrative assistant at an assisted living facility in Surrey, British Columbia. Vaincourt brings exotic birds to work with her. "Many people have had pets all their lives and then aren't able to bring them into a nursing facility," Vaincourt explained. "Having animals in the facility can help ease that loss. It's also a great way to get residents socializing. They'll open up and talk more."

She told Schipman about a recent resident who was having great difficulties adjusting to her new situation. "The woman had been here for about a week and hadn't really talked to anyone, didn't like coming down to the community area for activities or leaving her room for meals. One day I brought in an African grey parrot... It reminded her of the parrot she and her husband used to have. You could see the light come on in her and she started talking to other patients and the staff. Now she comes down every day to see what bird I may have brought in that day."

Even more unusual pets can have similar effects. Lavinia Stevens raises llamas on southern Vancouver Island, near Victoria, British Columbia. She takes her pure-white llama Wallace to visit residents in hospitals, nursing homes, and seniors' residences.

Wallace stands 6'2" tall. "He wanders in in his lordly style," says Stevens. "First people smile. Then they want to touch him, to stroke his neck."

One resident, severely debilitated by Alzheimer's disease, had not spoken an intelligible word in weeks. When she learned Wallace's name, she stood up and recited all five verses of Robbie Burns' poem, which begins,

> Scots, wha hae wi' Wallace bled,
> Scots, wham Bruce has aften led,
> Welcome to your gory bed
> Or to victorie!

As she concluded, she looked around and said, clearly, "I didn't know I still knew that!"

Therapy animals work, Lavinia Stevens suggests, "because people are not worried about what they say." A pet is not going to criticize them for forgetting details or getting their grammar tenses mixed up. The relationship matters, not the words.

Bruce and Sandy Sydnam also raise llamas and alpacas. "Sometimes we come back grumpy after a difficult day at work," Bruce admits. "Going out to feed the animals just feels like another thing demanding our attention. But by the time we come back in, we're much calmer and more content. They have that effect on us."

If you've watched horses in a parade, you may wonder how llamas fare on carpets in nursing homes. "They're very clean animals, naturally," says Lavinia Stevens. "They have one part of the pasture that's their poop pile. I take Wallace to it, he does his job, and then he will hold it for three hours while he's visiting."

Wallace's ministry of healing was featured in a documentary on *Healing with Animals*, by West Vancouver's Mary Bissell. Another episode focused on a healing pig. Priscilla Valentine had a history of grand mal epileptic seizures. But since a pot-bellied pig named Nellie became her constant companion, Valentine has been seizure-free.

"We all live hectic, stressful lives," says Bissell. "Pets provide a sense of normality. Animal therapy is not just anecdotal; it's backed up by science."

## Healing Effects

Many studies have shown that a few minutes spent with beloved pets can reduce blood pressure and muscle tension. Researchers reported to the American Heart Association, in 2005, that as little as a 12-minute visit with a friendly dog helped heart and lung function among hospitalized heart failure patients, by lowering blood pressure, reducing the release of harmful hormones, and decreasing anxiety. These benefits, they stated, exceeded those that resulted from a visit with a human volunteer, or from just being left alone.

"Animals bring out our nurturing instinct," explained another website. "They also make us feel safe and unconditionally accepted. We can just be ourselves around our pets."

Research has shown that heart attack victims who have pets live longer. A study of 92 patients hospitalized in coronary care units for angina or heart attack found that those who owned pets were more likely to be alive a year later than those who did not. The study found that only six percent of patients who owned pets died within one year, compared to 28 percent of those who did not own pets.

Even watching a tank full of tropical fish may lower blood pressure, at least temporarily. "People undergoing oral surgery," one report stated, "spent a few minutes watching tropical fish in an aquar-

*I am an animal lover, and working with my pets, I feel I make an important difference in the lives of people who are facing some serious challenges.*

– Gwen Meyer, pets for life program

ium. The subjects who watched the fish were more relaxed than those who did not watch the fish prior to the surgery…as calm as another group that had been hypnotized before the surgery."

I can't vouch for the accuracy of those unidentified studies, but I can vouch for the calming effect of watching tropical fish. While I was a student at university, afflicted with the usual raging hormones of that age group, I took care of a friend's tropical fish collection for most of a year. Waking in the middle of the night to the pale glow of the aquariums and the slow movements of the colourful fish almost always soothed my troubled mind.

I like to be on time for appointments, though I hate standing around waiting. A local restaurant has a large fish tank at its entrance; I'm always surprised how quickly time passes when I have to wait there.

Tim Faller, who edited this book, tells me that his mother-in-law has an aquarium in her living room. She would probably not describe herself as a spiritual person. But there's deep emotion in her voice when she says, "I like to just sit here and watch my fish swim."

The choice of animal doesn't seem to matter, says Sadey Guy, founder of the Pacific Animal Therapy Society (PATS), in Victoria. "We have some corn snakes that visit children in schools. We've had rabbits, guinea pigs, and even a macaw working with us. What's important is that your pet is an animal that really likes people and is good around people."

The late Dr. Bruce Hatfield loved to tell about a man named Archie. Archie was over 80, existing in a seniors' home in Toronto. He got a day

*Through the days of love and celebration and joy, and through the dark days of mourning – the faithful horse has been with us always.*

– ELIZABETH COTTON, FOLK MUSICIAN

pass to go and visit his daughter. But instead of going to his daughter's house, he caught a plane to Calgary, Alberta, and signed up with a group called Trail Riders of the Canadian Rockies. He spent a week riding a horse and camping in the wilderness, doing all the things that the staff at his nursing home said he wasn't supposed to do – and certainly wasn't considered capable of doing.

Bruce had absolutely no doubt that Archie's intimate contact with that horse for a week renewed his vitality, his joie de vivre.

All these examples are relatively passive. The llamas, the pigs, the fish don't actually *do* anything – they promote healing simply by their presence. But there are also animals whose actions are crucial to human survival. We've all seen guide dogs on the streets, enabling blind people to navigate crowded sidewalks and busy intersections. Other dogs assist people with physical challenges in their homes, or even work alongside the police to serve and protect.

## RESTORING SELF-RESPECT

"Our dogs do almost anything," says Sue Meinzinger, of Anacortes, near Seattle, Washington. Mostly, her Summit Dogs business trains service dogs. "They pull people in wheelchairs. They retrieve fallen items. They get the phone. They open doors. They become life partners. Some of them can even recognize medical problems, like anticipating someone's seizure before it happens, or recognizing a cancer growing."

*There is something about the outside of a horse that is good for the inside of a man.*

– SIR WINSTON CHURCHILL

Sue Meinzinger put me in touch with Sandi Larsen, who lives on an island near Seattle with her service dog, Thor. Larsen spends most of her life in a wheelchair. "If I drop something like a pen or a hairbrush," she says, "Thor picks it up and brings it back to me." Larsen has no left arm, so Thor also helps her get dressed and undressed.

"I have a poor sense of balance," she continues. "Sometimes, when I bend over, I fall out of my chair and can't get up. Thor brings me the telephone, so I can call 9-1-1."

Once, when she fell, her body blocked the phone, so that Thor could not reach it. On his own, Thor figured out how to turn the doorknob on the front door. Then he ran to her son's house across the road and barked until the son came to Larsen's rescue.

But perhaps most important of all, Thor helps Larsen feel like a person. When she's alone in her wheelchair, in public, "People act like I'm invisible," she says. But with Thor along, they often stop to talk to the dog first, and then get into conversation with his owner, too.

Marie Blythe owns another of Sue Meinzinger's service dogs. Blythe was severely disabled a few years ago by a car crash. Her dog, Gusto, brings her purse to her, gets out credit cards for clerks in stores, helps her load clothes into the dryer and take them out again… But as with Sandi Larsen, Gusto's most important function may be emotional. "He makes me feel good about myself," says Blythe. "He gives me some self-respect again."

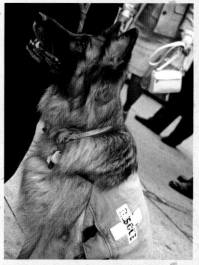

*My dogs give unconditional love, and they have taught me how to love unconditionally also. They go into a hospital room and look past the burn-scarred face of a man to his very heart and soul. With the wag of its tail, the dog says, "I love you – unconditionally."*

– Gwen Meyer, Pets for Life Program

"My real interest is not just dogs, but the human/animal relationship," says Professor Stanley Coren, a University of British Columbia professor who combines the study of human and dog psychology. Coren suggests that for people in power, a dog may be the only honest relationship they have. "They never betray you. They never sell their story to the *National Enquirer*."

Scott Yates wrote the article about Coren for the UBC alumni magazine, *Trek*. "We can deliberately manipulate dogs, and it doesn't take long," Coren told him. "In 10 or 12 years, you can completely change the breed."

One such change, Yates mused, has been to create dogs who have "a remarkable ability to understand and share our feelings. In other words, we have created dogs with empathy. Just as God is said to have created man in his image, we have created dogs in ours, revealing, in most cases, a reflection of the most honest, loyal, and affectionate parts of ourselves."

# 8
# Beyond the Box

PERHAPS PETS ARE TO HUMANS AS HUMANS ARE TO GOD

One night, Joan was home alone when she heard the back door rattle. At first, she thought it might be me coming in. But the door didn't open. Then she wondered if somebody might be delivering something. But the doorbell hadn't rung.

Just the doorknob, rattling.

With images from Alfred Hitchcock's horror movies racing through her mind, she peeked out. There was no one. No one at all.

As she stood there, the doorknob rattled again.

Finally, Joan mustered enough courage to stick her face right up against the door window. There, standing on his hind feet and swatting the doorknob with a front paw, was our large, black-and-white cat, Sylvester.

I suspect that Sylvester's intelligence compares to ours at roughly the same proportion as our intelligence to God's. Even if I had taken that door handle apart, and carefully explained to him exactly how all the different parts meshed to release the catch and open the door, Sylvester would never have understood.

In the same way, even if God could slow down the universe, could show us how all these stars and planets and atoms and molecules, all

*Only animals were not expelled from Paradise.*

-MILAN KUNDERA

111

these plants and animals and people, all mesh together into a coherent pattern of life and death and new life, we could never grasp it. Like the biblical Job, awestruck before God, we would have to admit that these are "things I do not understand, things too wonderful for me to know."

Yet somehow Sylvester recognized that the door handle had something to do with opening the door. Swatting the doorknob became a kind of ritual – and lo and behold, the door would open. Not always, but often enough to establish a connection.

Like Sylvester, we discover that there are special times when doors seem to open into God's presence. We sense that presence powerfully when we welcome new members into our families – in the birth of a child, or in marriage. We feel that God is somehow present when we gather in harmony around the table. We recognize God's comforting presence in the agony of grief. Not always. But often enough to know that it's possible.

And because we long for those moments, we create rituals to encourage them to happen again. So we come together to celebrate baptism, communion, marriage… In a sense, we rattle God's doorknobs. And lo and behold, sometimes the door opens.

The danger lies in assuming that we open the door – to grace, to love, to community, or to healing – through performing our rituals. We don't. Like Sylvester, we only rattle the doorknob. God opens the door.

Living with pets reminds us constantly of the disparity between their intelligence and ours – and thus of the disparity between us and God. As the prophet Isaiah quoted God: "My thoughts are not like

yours, and my ways are different from yours. As high as the heavens are above the earth, so high are my ways and thoughts above yours."

So every time I see my pets learning something about living with me, I see ways in which we can learn about living with God.

## The Law of the Leash

After we adopted Brick, Joan checked the encyclopedia to see what it said about Irish setters. "Require great patience to train," it told us. We discovered that immediately.

At the SPCA, we signed a promise that we would not let Brick run free for at least a year. So I made him a leash, and started taking him for walks. Brick embodied Murphy's Law; if there was a way to get his leash tangled, he would do it. The longer the leash, the more opportunity to get into trouble.

One day, he climbed a bank above the road, and dived under some old strands of barbed wire abandoned by a long-ago farmer. I called him back. He leaped over the wire. Struggling frantically, he fell down the bank and brought barbed wire, leash, and several uprooted bushes on top of me. While I tried to disentangle him, he wrapped the leash around my ankles and dumped me into the ditch.

Still, he learned from his experience. He never went near barbed wire again. He also learned – slowly – what I called the law of the leash. That is, if you go around the wrong side of a telephone pole, fire hydrant, or tree trunk, you will soon come to a very abrupt stop. And the faster you're running, the harder the stop.

The solution, from my perspective as the leash-holder, is simple. Brick simply had to retrace his steps to the point where he went wrong, make a different choice, and start over on the right side.

Brick's first inclination, though, is to pull harder. His second inclination is to expect me to bail him out. Unfortunately, then we usually both end up in trouble. We've gone around a neighbor's rose bush four times – me trying to unwind him, him dutifully following my footsteps and rewinding us both.

Brick acts very like the human race, I reflect. When we humans get into trouble, we tend, like Brick, to do the same thing that got us into trouble, only harder. Youth programs, education, law and order, morality, family values – when things go wrong, our answer is more of the same.

Similarly we expect God – or fate, or a lottery ticket – to bail us out. I don't suggest that God keeps us on a leash. But I do believe that God gives us as much freedom as possible. And so, when we get into trouble, the cause may lie generations back.

## Going Wrong

During my university days, a student in my residence had a pet raven. Unlike Edgar Allan Poe's raven, it did not say, "Nevermore." But it did almost everything else that it shouldn't have.

You have to understand that the corvid family – ravens, crows, magpies – is probably second only to the parrots for intelligence. Three scientists (Alex Weir, Jackie Chappell, and Alex Kacelnik) startled the world by showing that a crow named Betty could deliberately bend a straight piece of wire into a hook to retrieve food. Until then, it was taken for granted that only humans could *make* tools for themselves. Chimpanzees sometimes *used* tools, like twigs and piece of grass that they stuck in holes to collect grubs, but even they had never *created* a tool.

This raven had the intelligence to get into trouble. It wrecked the student's room – shredded his sheets, dismantled his radio, turned on his taps. It was also utterly ruthless, slaughtering a seagull that ventured onto the window sill. Eventually, the residence management issued an ultimatum: either the raven went, or the student did.

That raven taught me that intelligence alone cannot keep one from wrongdoing.

*If men had wings and bore black feathers, few of them would be clever enough to be crows.*

– Henry Ward Beecher, mid-1800s

*I have found that when you are deeply troubled there are things you get from the silent devoted companionship of a dog that you can get from no other source.*

– DORIS DAY, ACTRESS

# Hanging In

But it took one of our cats to teach me about forgiveness.

Lucky has a raspy little tongue, and she will lick anything – my hand, my shirt, my beard. I have even been wakened in the middle of the night by her licking my toes when they stuck out from under the covers, an experience that is hard to describe if you haven't actually had it happen.

I used to think that her licking was a sign of affection. One night, I realized it can be more like a plea for forgiveness.

Lucky doesn't like to be touched unexpectedly, especially on her hindquarters or belly. That night, she dozed in my lap as I worked at my computer. I needed to adjust her position. I slipped my hand under her, to move her. Waking instantly, she lashed out, hissing, slashing with bared claws, teeth poised to sink into my thumb.

Then, just as instantly, she realized she was in no danger. So she started licking my hand in what I took to be an apology for her hasty reaction.

If I had jerked my hand away, I could not have received her apology. Withdrawing my hand would have been the instinctive thing to do – little cats have sharp claws, and even sharper teeth. But that would have also taken me out of reach of her desire for reconciliation.

I wish I had understood that a few months earlier when a member of our community felt people had turned against her. As often happens in such instances, the woman withdrew into the safety of isolation. At the same time, her house sold. She left, without ever knowing that her friends and associates still respected and valued her.

To forgive and to be forgiven, we have to take the risk of continuing to be vulnerable. Forgiveness and reconciliation only happen to those who hang in long enough to receive it.

## The Process of Learning

In his book *The Far Side of Reason*, my father, William Taylor, argued that science and faith both depend on hypotheses that can be tested and proved. The difference is time. Science tests its theories in the lab. The results may take seconds, minutes, hours, weeks, or even months to prove. Faith experiments, on the other hand, are tested in people's lives. So the results take generations.

Some of our social problems began with the Vietnam War, some with colonialism, some with the Industrial Revolution, some with the ancient Greeks... Like Brick on his leash, we have to learn to retrace our steps until we figure out where we went wrong. Then we can launch ourselves forward again, on the right course. Brick only had to retreat a few steps; we may have to go back a few centuries. Any other course simply tangles us deeper and deeper.

For reasons that have little to do with his leash, but a lot to do with his scatterbrained personality, Brick severely tested his welcome

during his first months with us. We didn't know, at the time we got him from the SPCA, that he wasn't housebroken. And I don't mean just being trained to go outside for his personal emergencies. He knew nothing about living in a house, period. He chewed through the sleeve of my leather jacket. He tore the back off my Bible. He showered through the house the contents of the compost pail, the bucket of fireplace ashes, and a whole box of loose-leaf manuals for a workshop I was supposed to teach the next day.

One day we came home to find that he had torn open a 2 lb bag of flour, and dragged it through the house. He left a trail of flour two inches deep on the carpet. Then he was so happy to see us, he rolled in it, ecstatically wagging his long plumed tail.

I have to say, in Brick's favour, that he never made the same mistake twice. Except for the compost pail, that is, which seemed to hold a particular fascination for him. Otherwise, once we got through to him that he was not to chew up a ruler, he never touched it again. He chewed up my socks instead.

It took him about three months to learn that "No" didn't refer merely to the fireplace matches, Joan's pantyhose, or the TV remote control. No meant "none of the above." Ever. That's a big step for a dog. He has to develop general principles from specific instances.

It's a big step for humans, too, though we're supposedly blessed with much more reasoning power. There are humans – lots of them – who take individual incidents just as literally as Brick did. So they clean up garbage in their own yards, but don't expand that notion to our atmosphere. Businesses depend on customer loyalty, but don't reciprocate with loyalty to their employees. The values that people proclaim for home and family don't make it to the car lot and the boardroom.

Our world continually confronts us with new situations that have no precedents. There's nothing in the Bible, for example, to help us deal with hijackers, nuclear wastes, or telephone solicitation. Rather, we have to extrapolate from our existing knowledge, extending rules defined for specific situations into general principles applicable in a variety of different contexts. Like Brick, we have to figure out the broader meanings for ourselves.

If a dog can do it, why do humans have so much trouble?

*I think we are drawn to
dogs because they are the
uninhibited creatures we
might be if we weren't
certain we knew better.*

– GEORGE BIRD EVANS,
*TROUBLES WITH BIRD DOGS*

*Dogs are miracles with paws.*

— ATTRIBUTED TO SUSAN ARIEL RAINBOW KENNEDY

## Wishful Thinking?

The Christian tradition places a lot of faith in the Easter Resurrection. I don't know if it happened the way the Bible describes it. But I do know that whenever someone – human or animal – has mattered deeply to us, we desperately want to believe that it's not all over, that there is still something more to look forward to.

Our first dog, our first pet, was a terrier named Mickey. He barked at anyone wearing a uniform; everyone else he greeted with exuberant goodwill. Like every terrier, he believed he could beat up any dog bigger than himself. So he got to know the vet's office quite well. We took him there often to have his wounds repaired. He had more stitches than a hockey player's face.

When Mickey was about five, I got transferred to a job in a different city. The only accommodation available was an apartment, which did not allow any pets. We couldn't take Mickey. Nor could we imagine any other family owning him. So we left Mickey with my parents. They took him for his last visit to the vet. Mickey pranced into that familiar territory, sure that he was going to meet us again.

With all my heart, I hope that he was right. In the same way that I hope we will meet our beloved cat Tuppence again. And my mother, and my father in law, and our son Stephen…

If Mickey were still alive, he would be almost 50 years old, and Tuppence would be closing in on 40. If that age were even possible, both would be hopelessly decrepit. By the time I die, I may be equally infirm. But I see no reason why, if there is some kind of life after death, that Mickey and Tuppence – and our parents, our children, our friends – can't find us at the age and condition they loved best.

If time ceases to exist in eternity, then surely we are no longer limited to a single specific time. We can exist in two, or three, or any number of ages at once. Then, indeed, death would be no more.

At this point, I probably need to confess my own biases about death, and life after death, and resurrection. When my mother died at the age of 70, I was absolutely convinced that there was a life after death. I was sure she was living the familiar words of John's gospel: "I go before you, to prepare a place for you…"

When our son, Stephen, died of cystic fibrosis at 21, I was no longer so sure. If throwing myself down a stairwell or diving through an eighth-floor window would have saved his life, I would have done it without hesitation. But a nagging suspicion inside me said that it would just mean Joan had two deaths to cope with instead of one.

When my father – a minister and professor of theology, with three honorary Doctorates of Divinity – was dying at 93, I asked him what hymns and readings he wanted at his memorial service. "I don't care," he said. "I won't be there." But he did later ask that we scatter his ashes on his favourite fishing river.

So I simply don't know anymore. I'm content to wait and see. And whatever happens will be all right. But in the meantime, each death, each near death – whether it be a relative, a friend, or a pet – prods me to think more about the nature of God.

Like the weekend that Brick suffered peritonitis. I wasn't paying much attention. I had gone to bed with a miserable cold, sleeping or dozing until Sunday morning. I was just conscious enough that weekend to realize that Brick was very restless. He paced. He panted. He hovered near my head, or my feet, or slumped on the floor beside me. Every time I opened my eyes, I found his soft brown eyes staring into mine. Sunday morning, he even crawled up beside me.

In my self-centred stupor, I thought, "Isn't that sweet? He cares about me." It never occurred to me that Brick might need some care of his own. That in his restless pacing, he was trying to get us to pay attention to something going wrong with him.

*Dogs' lives are too short. Their only fault really.*

— AGNES SLIGH TURNBULL, AUTHOR

127

By Monday morning, it was clear – even as I milked the last dregs of sympathy for myself – that Brick was in trouble. We took him to the vet.

The vet gave us the verdict. "This is a very sick dog." The only hope was surgery. Immediately. Brick had less than a 50 percent chance of surviving until the operation. If he lived that long, he had less than a 50 percent chance of surviving the night. The alternative was euthanasia.

"What's your choice?" the vet asked.

Brick's eyes, now listless and dull, watched me steadily. Tears streamed into my beard as I held Brick in my arms. The vet injected sedation. Brick raised his head briefly, snuffled my face, and collapsed. The vet found a ruptured duodenal ulcer in Brick's small intestine. He removed the ulcer, sutured the wound, flushed the infected abdomen, and stitched up a raw red incision the length of the dog's belly.

All through that endless night and the following morning, I raged at God. I wanted to know what kind of God would deliberately inflict suffering on an innocent creature? Irish setters are among the gentlest, happiest dogs known. They hold no grudges; they have no mean streak whatsoever.

Others ask the same question when a child develops leukemia, when a father's brain dissolves with Creutzfeldt-Jakob disease, when an earthquake crushes 15,000 in India or 800,000 are massacred in Rwanda, or six million perish in Nazi death camps…

If an all-knowing, all-powerful God won't stop these heartbreaking events, doesn't that make God at least a collaborator in causing suffering? I cannot   I will not   believe in such a God.

*When you have an animal, you know you will say goodbye to that animal at some point.*

– JULIA BARR, ACTRESS

128

When I was a child, I'm sure I was cruel to other children — and they to me – often unintentionally, sometimes deliberately. As a young man, I felt contempt for those who failed to measure up to my standards or abilities. But I have, I hope, outgrown those attitudes. Through often painful experience, I have learned to be more compassionate, more tolerant, more understanding.

Why then should I worship a distant and indifferent God? Any God worth worshipping must give me something to aspire to. If I can weep over a dog's suffering, surely God must agonize even more over the losses in India or Rwanda.

Traditional marriage vows still say, "For better or for worse, for richer or for poorer, in sickness and in health…" When you love someone, you open yourself to sharing their hurt, their pain.

But the other side of that equation is that you can also share in rejoicing.

The morning after the operation, we went to visit Brick, not even sure if he was still alive. But in spite of an intravenous tube in his foreleg and stitches from his groin to his breastbone, he struggled groggily to his feet. The whole staff in the veterinary clinic crowded around to see the miracle. Then Brick took a short and very wobbly few steps.

I'd like to think that God's heart overflowed with joy. Certainly mine did.

*There is no greater pleasure than having a dog. And that's a scientific fact!*

– LOUIS SABIN, COMMENTING ON A UNIVERSITY STUDY ON THE EFFECT OF OWNING A DOG

129

*Those who wish to pet and baby wild animals "love" them.*
*But those who respect their nature and wish to let them live normal lives,*
*love them more.*

– EDWIN WAY TEALE, *CIRCLE OF SEASONS*, 1954

# 9
# A Living Mirror

SEEING OURSELVES REFLECTED IN OUR PETS

I had brought home a bag of small wind-up toys from my local thrift shop. Some of them worked, some didn't. I hoped to repair those that were salvageable. I put the bag down while I went to do something else.

With the curiosity typical of cats, Mush poked inside to see if there was anything there to play with. She must have pawed a toy that was fully wound up, just waiting to activate. Mush exploded out of the bag – unfortunately, through one of the hand holes. Looped around her neck, the bag pursued her. Mush fled through the house, leaving behind a trail of little mechanical toys, buzzing, beeping, squawking, walking, rotating…

We found Mush cowering behind the couch, trembling, while the last of the toys unwound itself in the remains of the plastic bag that still hung around her neck.

We humans might argue that if she had just stayed still, no harm would have come to her, and we could easily have disentangled her from the bag. But panic doesn't work that way.

It doesn't work that way in people, either. People who are scared, who feel threatened, react in unpredictable ways. We don't pay enough

131

attention to our fears. We acknowledge other motivations – greed, guilt, generosity, altruism, cynicism – but we don't recognize, or are unwilling to admit, the extent to which our fears push our buttons.

Even in places that promote compassion and sensitivity, such as our places of worship, if we feel threatened, we react. We lash out – at same-sex marriage, at changes to prayer books and hymnals, at a picture of a black Jesus…

## Threatened by Change

There is so much change going on these days that almost everyone feels threatened in one way or another. My friend John Towgood sees the traditional teachings of his church being re-interpreted for a modern context. He worries, "I'm afraid we may throw the baby out with the bathwater." When fellow church members discover new metaphors, new images, new understandings of God, he challenges, "But what about sin? What about forgiveness? What about the Trinity?"

At times of change, we can learn from the way our pets struggle with it.

132

Brick, for example, became bewildered when the rules he thought he understood changed. He discovered early in his life that if he yelped at the back door to come in, instead of scratching the door, he not only got let into the house, he got a cookie for speaking to us about his needs. Then he realized he could use this process to get more cookies. First he went to the door and asked to go out. Then he turned right around and asked to come back in.

But all those cookies weren't good for him. So we changed the rules. We still opened the door. We patted him and stroked him and assured him he was a good dog. But no cookie. He couldn't understand what had gone wrong.

Brick was experiencing, in his own small way, what's happening to all of us. The old order changes, and we feel as if we're trying to walk on quicksand. Old values, old standards, old commitments – they're all up for grabs, open to negotiation.

Brick suffered from a common delusion: he assumed that rules were permanent. In fact, his rules had been changing all along. They changed when he learned to yelp, instead of scratch. They changed when he got a cookie, instead of just getting in. But until this last change, they always changed for his benefit.

That's why most of us get upset, too. For the last century or more, most of the rules have worked in our favour. Cars gave us mobility, industries gave us prosperity, and technology gave us leisure time. Now technology threatens to give us unemployment, cars clog our roads and pollute our air, and industries poison our environment.

Like Brick, we find the rules changing. It's a new world, and we're not sure we like it.

## Reward and Punishment

When I was younger, parents took for granted that spanking their children was an acceptable way to teach discipline. The Bible even says, "Spare the rod and spoil the child." But I suspect almost everybody now knows that beating children is not the best way to raise them.

Severe discipline doesn't work with pets, either. But neither, I'm discovering, does simply rewarding them.

When we got our dog Phoebe, she was somewhat erratic at coming when called. Sometimes she came; sometimes she shrugged and went on doing her own thing. So I started carrying doggie treats with me. Now she comes galloping when I whistle. Not because that's the right thing to do, but because she wants her reward.

Reward and punishment have the same teaching value. They don't really teach right and wrong – or if they do, that understanding comes much later. Rather, they teach us to want the reward, and to avoid the penalty.

That lust for rewards seems clearer in animals than in our own behaviour. My family was enjoying a picnic lunch in the parking lot at Mount Edith Cavell, in Jasper National Park. As soon as food came out, insolent Canada jays descended upon us. They strutted around on the ground. They perched on the car's trunk lid. They landed on the picnic table.

We tossed them a few scraps from our store-bought sandwiches. With great disdain, they turned the scraps over with their beaks – and waited for something better. I don't know how they knew we had chocolate chip cookies tucked away. But as soon as those cookies came out of their sealed container, the birds got so bold they would peck pieces right out of our hands.

Author Keith Wright suggests that our obsession with reward and punishment distorts traditional understandings of heaven and hell. We aren't good because goodness leads to a better, more satisfying life – we're good so that we can get our reward in heaven. Similarly, we avoid being bad because we don't want to go to hell. Surely it would be better if we simply wanted to do good, for its own sake – whatever we may believe about an eternal hereafter.

When I read books and magazines about training pets, one message comes through over and over. The idea is not to make them afraid of their masters. Nor is it to get pets to think of their masters as bottomless pits of tasty treats.

It's easy, for example, to train squirrels or raccoons to come for snacks. We once did that with a mother squirrel. We called her "Mama." She soon learned to take peanuts from our fingers. A year later, a squirrel who looked vaguely familiar bounced across our lawn. "I wonder if

that's Mama," said Joan. At the sound of her name, the squirrel spun around and ran up to us for her treat.

We were fortunate. Mama never presumed that she had a right to be fed. Some acquaintances weren't so lucky. They had trained some squirrels to come to the kitchen window of their summer cottage. When the free lunch program ended in September, the squirrels bit through the window screen, chewed through the window frame, and just about destroyed the kitchen to get at the food they considered themselves entitled to.

Our next door neighbours discovered how raccoons can outsmart humans. They were having a barbecue one evening. A mother raccoon and three young ones paraded across the bottom of the yard, next to the back fence. The humans all crowded around for a better view of their animal visitors. Even the chef left his barbecue long enough to watch the family parade. He turned around just in time to see papa raccoon heading down the driveway with one of his steaks.

The better alternative, pet magazines tell me, is to train the pet to want to please its owner. Horses and dogs are perhaps most likely to respond to this motivation; cats, least likely. I have had little experience with horses myself, but friends tell me that when they build rapport with a horse, they rarely need bridle, reins, or even saddle to control their mount. Horse and rider become a single, indivisible unity.

Which is, in fact, a deeply religious concept. Believers do what God wants, not to gain a reward or avoid punishment, but simply to please their invisible partner.

*Closeness, friendship, affection: keeping your own horse means all these things.*

— BERTRAND LECLAIR, AUTHOR

137

The problem is often not so much our ability to choose, as our all-or-nothing mindset. We feel that something has to be either one thing or the other – either good or bad – but never both/and. So if I disagree with his religious teachings about original sin, I have to reject all of St. Augustine's thinking.

But the deer that nibble in my garden tell me that's not so.

Most urban dwellers would give up their birthright to watch a herd of deer gently browsing in their gardens in the early half-light of dawn. They move with the fluidity of oil; their eyes are big and soft; their coats ripple... They are so beautiful.

They are also so destructive. Because they have just finished nipping off every rosebud in our garden. All around us, the farmers have put up eight-foot deer fencing to protect their crops. Our rural road now resembles the perimeter of a medium-security penitentiary. Unable to munch their way through the orchards anymore, the deer treat our gardens like a salad bar.

We had no tulips this spring. The deer ate them all.

We had no roses last year. The deer ate them all.

Cedar hedges are supposed to grow tall and straight. All the hedges in our neighbourhood have distinct hourglass figures. Tender new cedar branches are the hors d'oeuvres before the deer snack on our struggling little dogwood sapling.

I am not a hunter. I succumbed years ago to Walt Disney's adorable little Bambi. But I must admit that when I see another rosebush cropped back, when the lawn mower redistributes another pile of deer droppings, when I have to protect every planting with unsightly chicken wire, I'm strongly tempted to savour a venison dinner.

How can deer be two things at once? Both beautiful and destructive? Both desired and despised? The problem is our thinking patterns, not the deer. We demand consistency. Something must be *either* this, *or* that – it can't be both.

You can see that conviction applied everywhere. The coach who was the fans' darling last year is this year's scapegoat. A politician goes overnight from white knight to wicked witch. The new spouse who seemed perfect in every way suddenly has irritating mannerisms that make you dream of divorce…

We should learn from life itself. Every experience has both good and bad elements. Our most fundamental needs — breath, water, warmth, community — can also be the most hazardous. Our challenge is not to choose one or the other of contradictory extremes, but to pick a delicate path between extremes. To tiptoe through the tulips, in a sense – if the deer have left any.

*The world has different owners at sunrise… Even your own garden does not belong to you. Rabbits and blackbirds have the lawns; a tortoise-shell cat who never appears in daytime patrols the brick walls, and a golden-tailed pheasant glints his way through the iris spears.*

– ANNE MORROW LINDBERGH, AUTHOR

139

*There are two things for which animals are to be envied: they know nothing of future evils, or what people say about them.*

– VOLTAIRE

We all tend to go to extremes, without realizing what we're doing. Extremes look silly when someone else does them. Especially when something that we consider a lesser order of creation does them.

We had a cat, for example, who held grudges. When we went away on holidays, we usually contracted with our paper boy – who was also a member of my Scout group – to come in twice a day to feed Tuppence. He did far more. Morning and evening, he'd sit and chat with her, rub her ears, and brush her. Tuppence loved it. If he let her out, he always came back during the day to let her back in again. She didn't lack anything. She thrived on his attention.

But she wasn't getting that attention from us. So when we returned, she made us pay. One time, we were unloading the car when I saw Tuppence up the street. I called her. At the sound of my familiar but long-missing voice, she whirled and started running – yes, actually running – towards me.

And then she stopped. Stopped dead. And turned. And stalked away, tail in the air.

It was as if she had thought, "Wait a minute! These are the people who abandoned me for three weeks. Why should I reward them by being friendly? Let them suffer for a while…" Tuppence had an excellent sense of timing. She treated us coldly for almost exactly the length of time that we had ignored her by being on holidays.

She reminds me of people who hold grudges. They pattern their lives on the Old Testament maxim: "An eye for an eye, and a tooth for a tooth." If they've been snubbed, they snub in return. If they've been slighted, they disparage back. If they've been hurt, they keep the wound open. It's not quite revenge. Revenge sounds too formal, too planned, too vindictive. But it's not very different.

Someone explained to me once that every religion has its own unique quality. For Islam, it's obedience – submission to the will of God. For Hinduism, reincarnation – earning your way into higher levels of life. Judaism, this person suggested, was founded on a legal code defined by Moses in the desert – it focused on personal righteousness.

I don't know how accurate his definitions were for other religions, but I did like the emphasis he chose for Christianity – forgiveness.

Jesus made some extraordinary claims, so extraordinary they infuriated the religious authorities of his time. "Your sins are forgiven," he told people, knowing that according to his religious traditions, both forgiveness and vengeance were reserved for God. His last words before dying on the cross, one of the gospels tells us, included, "Forgive them, for they know not what they do."

He told his followers to forgive others, not just once, not just seven times, but seventy times seven. And not merely to forgive those who had wronged them, but to love them, to turn the other cheek, even to give up their lives for them.

There is no room for grudges in such a philosophy.

*All animals except man know that the*
*ultimate [point] of life is to enjoy it.*

— Samuel Butler

# FUNNY STUFF

It helps if we can learn not to take ourselves so seriously.

Our cat Mush sat at the top of the stairs, one day. As she sometimes does, she started chasing her tail, sort of half heartedly. This time, though, she snagged a claw in her own tail. It hurt. She spat – at herself – and rotated more vigorously. One hind paw slipped over the edge of the top step. She tumbled down the stairs to the landing – thumpety-bump – still struggling with her own tail.

I laughed. I couldn't help it.

Mush extricated her claw, glared at me, and stalked off.

Later that day, I raced out of the house for an appointment. Or rather, I tried to race out. I grabbed my coat out of the closet and knocked two more coats onto the floor. Trying to pick the coats up, I knocked over an umbrella standing in the corner. It jammed when I tried to close the doors. I bent over to pick up the umbrella, and bashed my head on the partially opened closet door. As I reeled back from the blow, I tripped over the coat I had originally grabbed, and landed on my tailbone.

I looked up from my new position – on the floor – and realized Mush was watching me. She looked rather as if she might be grinning.

When our children were younger, I lectured about doing the household chores. Cleaning up the kitty litter was supposed to be their job. But it was starting to stink up the basement, and the cat was showing a distinct reluctance to use the litter box.

*When I play with my cat, who knows whether she isn't amusing herself with me more than I am with her?*

– MICHAEL DE MONTAIGNE,
RENAISSANCE SCHOLAR

143

Perhaps I was a little severe. To soften any harshness in my criticism, I decided to be a kindly father and help them with the chore. I held the garbage bag open while Stephen dumped the litter box into it. The bag had a hole in the bottom. The entire aromatic mess cascaded through onto my feet.

I don't think I ever saw Stephen laugh harder.

I told Joan about it that evening. She laughed, too.

"I knew you were going to laugh," I said ruefully.

"I'm sorry," she said, stifling her laughter for a few seconds, "but I couldn't help it." And she started laughing again.

## The Wisdom of Aging

As I grow older, I'm finding that annoyances fall into perspective. Mountains become molehills. Phoebe and Brick have both helped me realize that.

Both dogs are Irish setters, renowned for wandering off. But in their senior years, we could let them out into the yard without fearing they would immediately race onto the street. When I took Brick for a walk, he didn't try to chase a strutting pheasant through a barbed wire fence. When visitors came to our house, he no longer acted like a superball on steroids. And he didn't chew up Joan's gardening gloves for months.

He became a lot easier to live with. He was slower, of course. But he was also more placid, more patient. More gentle, less impetuous, more tolerant, less demanding.

I rather liked him that way.

In fact, as he aged, he became more like what I sometimes hope I can be.

Churches – and, I believe, religions in general – tend to inculcate certain virtues: patience, kindness, tolerance, love, acceptance... These are all virtues more commonly associated with the elderly than with the young. We expect young people to be energetic, vigorous, ambitious; to take risks; to push their limits. It's older folks who become more placid, more contented, more philosophical about the slings and arrows of outrageous fortune.

Not all of them, of course. I once interviewed an expert on geriatrics. She asserted that, "As we grow older, we become more like what we've always been, only more so." Even if that sentence defies rational analysis, its meaning is clear. Some people become increasingly crabby and miserable. Others grow kinder, more compassionate, more accepting of our shortcomings.

In his younger years, Brick believed that his mission in life was to catch ducks. He charged into the lake after them like a rampaging hippo, splashing and surging water everywhere. The ducks, naturally enough, took off.

One day he saw a flock of a dozen mergansers just off the shore. When he hit the water, they waggled their webbed feet underwater so hard and so fast that they whipped the water to a froth around themselves. They left a wake like a motorboat.

Brick had no more chance of catching them than he had of flying. He yelped and yowled at them to come back, that high-pitched yelp that says life is not fair. But catching ducks in the water is one goal he will never achieve. He's doomed to fail. Like most of us, I suspect.

Author May Sarton commented in one of her books that artists never achieve what they reach for. That's why they're artists – they're always trying to capture, in words or paint or music, an eternally moving target.

## ACCEPTING OUR LIMITATIONS

Does that mean, like Brick, we're doomed to be failures?

Did Jesus, charged with treason and executed, feel like a failure on the cross?

If the sum total of Jesus' life came to an end on the cross, he was hardly a model for success. Early in his ministry, he announced that he had come to free the prisoners, to give sight to the blind... At the end, there were a few more people who could see – but he didn't end blindness. There were a few more who could walk – but he didn't end crippling injuries or diseases. There's no record of him setting any prisoners free from their jails. He didn't even manage to save his relative, John the Baptist. And by the end, there was one more prisoner – Jesus himself.

His own disciples had run for cover, deserting him. He hadn't changed the belief system of his own disciples, let alone the Jewish people.

So it's quite possible that he felt like a failure.

"Is that all there is?" Peggy Lee asked in a song. If that's all there is, if even the human embodiment of God died a failure, then there is no hope for us.

But if there was some kind of resurrection on the third morning, then failure is not the end.

We may never accomplish all that we set out to do. There will certainly be unmended relationships, unfinished commitments, unachieved dreams when we die. But that is not necessarily the end, either. If we have lived a good life, and enjoyed as much of it as possible – as Brick, and Phoebe, and Tuppence all did – life has not been a failure.

*Nothing is more sacred than the bond between horse and rider...*
*no other creature can ever become so emotionally close to a human as a horse.*
*When a horse dies, the memory lives on because an enormous part of his owner's heart, soul, very existence dies also... but that can never be laid to rest, it is not meant to be...*

– STEPHANIE M. THORN

147

# 10
# At the End

If the animals in my life have taught me a lot about how to live, they have taught me even more about how to die.

The process of dying, for most of us humans, is a miserable business. "There has to be a better way of dying," my friend Ralph Milton said to me one day. He had just come back from visiting his sister. A heavy smoker most of her life, she was dying of emphysema. When he spoke to me, she was on oxygen, night and day. She had no energy, but couldn't sleep. A five-minute conversation would exhaust her for hours. She was miserable.

In desperation, she turned to alcohol. "It makes me feel better than the pills they give me," she told Ralph. And then, tellingly, she added, "I'm just trying to hurry up the end."

I remember my mother, destroyed by Hodgkin's lymphoma; my father, debilitated by a series of heart attacks; my son, reduced to a walking skeleton by cystic fibrosis; my stepmother, a prisoner of her dialysis equipment. None of them enjoyed their final months, perhaps their final years. They would cheerfully have gone much sooner.

At my father's lowest point, a hospital nurse tried to encourage him. "You have to keep trying," she said.

*There are two lasting bequests we can give our children: one is roots. The other is wings.*

- Hooding Carter, Jr.

149

"I'm too tired to keep trying," he gasped.

I took him in my arms. "Dad, if you want to go, it's okay," I told him.

He started sobbing. "I want to go," he blubbered. "I want to go."

But he couldn't. Not yet. Because his body could not break a 93-year habit of staying alive.

## Dying with Some Dignity

I could not have intervened to end the lives of any of those people I mentioned. But I'm not sure if my reluctance was about them, or about me. Because I did intervene when our dog Brick's collective infirmities finally left him collapsed in a heap, unable to get up, unable to do more than stare at me with pleading eyes.

We took him to the vet. I cradled his head in my arms as the vet injected the first dose of sedative. Brick sighed deeply, and the stress in his body relaxed. His eyes closed. He fell asleep. The second injection took

a few minutes to act. Brick took a final, quiet breath. His heart stopped. He passed away painlessly, without any struggle.

We humans rarely have that privilege. But I suspect that most of us would prefer to end our lives that way, rather than withering away in a hospital bed or a nursing home.

To be honest, I don't suppose that our presence made much difference to Brick by that time. I'm probably just projecting onto him my own feelings. I know that when my time runs out, I don't want to open my eyes in a final moment of lucidity, and feel alone, abandoned, unloved. So I guess I wanted to hold Brick in my arms, because I hope someone will do the same for me when my time comes.

Unfortunately, that opens the whole messy matter of euthanasia. Of fears that self-centred children might decide to dispose of elderly parents who have become inconvenient. Of fears that unscrupulous administrations could dispose of unwanted citizens – such as people with expensive disabilities, or ethnic groups, or political dissidents.

Of my personal fears that someone, somewhere, might decide that I am expendable.

I accept the argument that life is sacred. But I do not accept that ending life with dignity is playing God. We have already played God when we keep alive infants with no brain stems, when we perform multiple heart bypasses, when we vaccinate against infectious diseases, when we overwhelm infections with antibiotics. Having played God, we then force people to waste away miserably, no longer valuing the supposedly sacred life that refuses to let them go.

*I believe in God, only I spell it Nature.*

— FRANK LLOYD WRIGHT, ARCHITECT

*Our task must be to free ourselves... by widening our circle of compassion to embrace all living creatures and the whole of nature and its beauty.*

— ALBERT EINSTEIN

151

## Not with a Bang, But a Whimper

I have personally known only one person who died without any sense of withering away. At 63, my former boss Al Forrest had no symptoms of ill health, other than a tendency to wake up long before anyone else in his family was ready to rise.

"So get up and read a book," said his doctor.

That morning, he got out of bed while it was still dark, switched on the light behind his favourite easy chair, and sat down to read a favourite book. His family found him there several hours later, the light spilling down over his head, the book resting calmly in his lap.

Most of us go through a much longer process of decline and decay. Weakening health prevents us from doing things we used to enjoy. Our joints hurt. Our minds fail to function as well as they once did. Increasingly, our world narrows down to fewer and fewer close associates, until there's not much left to celebrate. Life, for many, turns into a long, drawn-out whimper.

I might accept this as the natural order of things. But my pets have shown me that it doesn't have to be that way.

Tuppence made it to almost 20. Mush is now 18. Spice reached 15 before arthritis so limited her movement that it was time to go. Phoebe is 13 as I write this, an unusual age for large, purebred dogs.

Brick's decline started when he was about eight – in dog years, close to my own age. Getting out of bed in the morning, he had to struggle to his feet. He stumbled going up or down stairs. When we went for walks, his gallop had turned into a trot; his trot had turned into a plod.

I recognized all these symptoms, because I have them myself.

## Peering into My Future

Watching old age develop in Brick was like watching a video running on fast forward. One year in a dog's life is roughly equivalent to seven to ten years of a human's life. Maybe more, if you're born an Irish setter, inbred for generations to produce that silky red coat, and a tendency to epilepsy and hip dysplasia. So once he was past his prime – like me

*I have developed a deep respect for animals. I consider them fellow living creatures with certain rights that should not be violated any more than those of humans.*

— JAMES STEWART, ACTOR

— what happened to him each year is what I can expect to happen to me over a longer period.

Like me, Brick kept believing he was younger than he really was. I drove a small sports car in an effort to cling to my youth. Brick, too, remembered being young and frisky. He still tried to leap up onto the top of the hot tub, where he could lie in the sunshine and lord it over lesser beings. Sometimes he made it. More often, he crashed onto the edge, winded himself, and hobbled away in shock.

Obviously, he remembered that he used to make that jump easily. That's why he still tried it. He could recognize the past – he just had trouble integrating it with the present.

But unlike Brick, I can anticipate the future. So I knew that watching Brick grow older was like getting a sneak peek at my own future.

## LAST WISHES

In his final weeks, I would have given almost anything to see Brick happy again. When he went racing through long grass, or pulled our underwear out of the laundry basket, or chased a Frisbee, he had a devil-may-care grin on his face.

When my father was fading away in a hospital bed, I desperately wished that he could have one last chance to stand in a mountain stream somewhere, fly fishing. I wanted him to have one last chance to send that luminous line arcing through the sunlight above emerald-green water, to feel the rush of adrenaline when a fish comes surging out of the water in a shower of glistening spray.

When my mother was dying, I wished she could be a hostess one last time. She loved having people in, setting the tables, bringing out the china and the tea services, getting everything just right.

As I think about these "last wishes," I find myself wondering why these seem so important to me. Perhaps it's because those who are dying have lost so much of themselves. And we who are left resent it. We're angry that those we love are so reduced from what they were.

And yet, and yet…

In my mother's final week, she made last-minute arrangements to dispose of her best china, so that it could continue to grace tables in other hostesses' homes.

In my father's final weekend, he took his granddaughter back to the apartment he used to live in. For one glorious afternoon, he handed over to her all his fly rods, his lines, his flies. He spent the hours explaining to her why each one was special, and how to use it. "I think he was reliving all those experiences," she said later.

And our dog's final voluntary act, before we took him to the vet's to begin a sleep from which he would not waken, was to steal my socks while I was having a shower. He could barely totter, but he stole my socks. I'm sure there was a grin on his face when I dug those socks out from under him.

Maybe we do get one last chance. Maybe it just doesn't come in the way we survivors imagine it.

*"I meant," said Ipslore bitterly, "what is there in this world that truly makes living worthwhile?"*
*Death thought about it.*
*"Cats," he said eventually, "cats are nice."*

Terry Pratchett, *Sourcery*

155

*We can only hope to achieve as humans, what comes so freely from our pets...unconditional love, loyalty and true companionship.*

– Darcy Bomford, 1987 founder, president and CEO of pet food/treat manufactory

Brick's decline and death was the most traumatic thing that happened to me that year. Before his death, I grieved for him. For his loss of mobility, of independence, of dignity. For the helpless, bewildered look in his eyes when his body no longer let him prance and play, when his legs collapsed after three tottering steps.

After his death, I grieved for me. For *my* losses. For not having a companion on walks. Indeed, not having an incentive to take walks. I missed his resonant "woof" when the doorbell rang, the thump-thump of his tail on the carpet when I came home. Most of all, I missed his unconditional affection.

About six months later, I was finally able to look back, to start mining his legacy of memories, to see what they might mean for me as a survivor.

Now I know that I learned from him, first, that going is more important than getting there. Brick didn't care how many times we walked the same route. For him, getting out mattered, not our destination. He didn't care how many times he caught a Frisbee, or, for that matter, how many times he didn't catch a squirrel.

I'm learning that I don't need a purpose, a goal, or an excuse for doing something worthwhile.

Second, I learned never to presume malice. Brick treated everyone and everything as a potential friend. He never started a fight with another dog, even if it approached with stiff legs and bared teeth. Until experience indicated otherwise, he assumed that every cat wanted its hindquarters snuffled. And that all humans were kindly. He wasn't always right. But he had a far better success rate than if he approached everyone with a hostile attitude.

So I'm learning to give people the benefit of the doubt, or at least not to start with prejudices against them.

Third, I learned that life without joy is no life at all. Perhaps only an Irish setter could teach that particular lesson, for Irish setters have a reputation for being the most playful of dogs. We humans often have trouble dealing with joy. Maybe we're afraid of it. It seems so uncontrolled. We humans desperately want to be in control – of ourselves, of each other, of our world.

I'm still learning from Brick that it doesn't all depend on me. I can step back, and let the universe unfold as it should.

Lastly, I'm learning from him that everything, in the end, boils down to relationships. Brick had no possessions. He was never elected leader of the pack. But he had wonderful relationships. He died knowing he was deeply loved.

I couldn't ask any more for myself.

*We give dogs time we can
spare, space we can spare
and love we can spare. And
in return, dogs give us their
all. It's the best deal man
has ever made.*

– M. Facklam